CW00820899

EAST OF ORPHANIDES

Also by George Lassalle

The Adventurous Fish Cook

Chasing the Chattel

Fish and Shellfish
(Sainsbury Classic Cookbooks)

The Fish in my Life
(published in paperback as
The Further Adventures of a Fish Cook)

EAST
OF
ORPHANIDES

My Middle Eastern Food

George Lassalle

KYLE CATHIE LIMITED

First published in Great Britain by
Kyle Cathie Limited
3 Vincent Square London SW1P 2LX

Copyright © Caroline Lassalle 1991

ISBN 1 85626 033 X

A CIP catalogue record for this book is available from
the British Library

All rights reserved. No reproduction, copy or transmission of
this publication may be made without written permission. No
paragraph of this publication may be reproduced, copied or
transmitted save with written permission or in accordance with
the provisions of the Copyright Act 1956 (as amended). Any
person who does any unauthorised act in relation to this
publication may be liable to criminal prosecution and civil
claims for damages.

Typeset by DP Photosetting, Aylesbury, Bucks
Printed and bound by Butler & Tanner Ltd
Frome and London

CONTENTS

Acknowledgements	vii
Introductory Note	ix
Middle Eastern Memories	1
Mezé	18
Soups	29
Eggs	41
Fish	48
Grains and Pulses	61
Vegetables and Salads	82
Meat and Chicken	124
Sauces and Dressings	157
The Sweet Course	164
Culinary Notes	177
Bibliography	189
Index	190

For Kylos,
always 'the onlie begetter'

ACKNOWLEDGEMENTS

M Y WARMEST THANKS for unfailing and generous help and advice to Soraya Antonius, Anne Cavendish, Androula Costi, Rebecca Savvides, Prue Seymour, Charles Snow, Maroula Zenonos and, above all, Meric Dobson. I must stress that none of these kind and clever people is responsible for any errors of mine.

Thanks to Alan Davidson for permission to include the extract from *A Kipper with My Tea* (Macmillan 1988, Papermac 1990) and the estate of the late Arto der Haroutunian for his recipes for Arab bread and for making and stabilizing yogurt from *Middle Eastern Cookery* (Century 1982, Pan Books 1983).

QUANTITIES

The recipes in this book serve 4 to 6 people.

INTRODUCTORY NOTE

THE SUBTITLE OF this book is not merely the pretext for an ego-trip. There are other reasons for the use of the possessive pronoun, 'my'.

Experts such as the brilliant and encyclopaedic Claudia Roden and the late, much-missed Arto der Haroutunian were introduced to Middle Eastern food in their cradles. Their intimate knowledge of it is supported by that of a network of relatives and friends also immersed in the traditions of the region. In addition, their impressive culinary research has been carried out in languages to which I have no access: Arabic, Turkish, Armenian and Hebrew.

My own modest qualifications for writing a book on this subject are quite different. Of my lifetime as a keen gastronome, cook and – for the past two decades – cookery writer, thirty years have been spent in various parts of the Middle East. During this time, I have formed preferences, the reasons for which may be of some interest. For, coming from outside the Middle Eastern tradition – brought up, though in England, to revere French and Italian cuisine – I have been free to pick and choose ... even, at times, to reject. I am not bound by the mystic ties of childhood associations and nostalgia. Such ties led Proust to transform a dusty little cake, 'dunked' in a *tisane*, into his immortal *madeleine*. It has occurred to me that Claudia Roden feels similar emotions about a bowl of little brown beans (*ful medammes*). I, on the other hand, am a mini-Columbus, sailing foreign seas.

The great culinary interest of my life has been fish. (I have written three books on the subject.) But despite this devotion, and my frequent adherence to a predominately fishy regimen, fish has never formed my entire diet. Especially during my years in the Middle East, where fish is often hard to find and ways of cooking it are limited, I have sampled – and cooked – many other kinds of food. I hope this account of experiences and discoveries in the Middle East will convey my enjoyment and enable others to share it.

An important point: there is no canon or 'rule' for Middle Eastern cookery as there is for classic French cuisine. Kitchen knowledge is transferred almost invariably from person to person by word of mouth, rather than through written records. And much variation occurs not only from region to region but from cook to cook. I have found those in the Middle East particularly unsympathetic to the giving of exact measurements and quantities in recipes. Surely, they must feel, this is a matter of individual tastes and needs?

I have, in accordance with modern culinary practice, tried to give quantities for most spices and herbs. But you are at liberty to disagree with me . . . and neither of us need be wrong. However, as far as salt and pepper are concerned, I have usually balked. I feel that a cook who flavours and seasons food without tasting it is like an actor putting on make-up without the help of a mirror. In both cases, the results are unsatisfactory. For heaven's sake, *taste* . . . and taste frequently. As far as I am concerned, this is an essential part of learning the art of Middle Eastern (and, for that matter, any other) cookery.

Finally, I would suggest that if you are interested in acquiring an 'idea' (albeit a simple one) of Middle Eastern cookery (as opposed to preparing one or two dishes), you should read through the Culinary Notes at the end of this book (pages 177–188) before embarking on the recipes.

George Lassalle
Limassol, 1991

MIDDLE EASTERN
MEMORIES

T HE ORPHANIDES BRASSERIE was superbly and uniquely placed in
the very middle of the fashionable district of Athens, a few
paces from the world-famous Grande Bretagne Hotel. They shared
the distinction of having broad surrounding pavements made of
finely bonded blocks of Pentelic marble from the same quarry that
originally supplied the material for the construction of the
Parthenon and its companion temples and shrines on the Acropolis.
Orphanides was within easy walking distance of most of the better
restaurants and places of entertainment, including the three
theatres which served food to accompany their satirical reviews.
These very pleasant places – the Aigli, the Oasis and the Pefka –
enjoyed the delightful shelter of the Zappeion Gardens.

Some account of my first scapegrace journey to Greece in 1933
appears in an earlier book of mine*, but nowhere did I express my
gratitude to the friends, Leonard Bower and Jim Tovey, who
introduced me to the varied delights of life in Athens nearly sixty
years ago. One of the legacies they left me was the habit of taking my
aperitifs, before lunch and dinner, at Orphanides.

Over the years, the Orphanides habit has provided me with many
reveries. It was not just a watering hole where I could be fairly
certain that my most favourite mezés would be available. It was a
peep-show at which I could observe what seemed to be all human

* *The Fish in My Life*, Macmillan 1989 (also entitled *The Further Adventures of a Fish
Cook*, Papermac, 1991)

life: from shoe-blacks, sometimes three to a customer, to pale Etonians, from distinguished-looking gangsters to battered-looking Balkan princes.

Sitting outside Orphanides, sipping ouzo and nibbling at small slices of *avgotarakho*, or scooping out the delicious *kidonia thalassina* (sea-quinces) offered by wandering vendors, I always felt as if I were at the very heart of Greece, taking part in the essential life of the country.

I was an obnoxious youth, with an ungovernable propensity to fall in love with every pretty girl or woman I met. And there was no shortage of beautiful young women in Athens, though they seemed to be considerably outnumbered by elegant young men.

It was not long, therefore, before Irene Freeman, who had originally drawn me abroad and then abandoned me for two others, a Swiss sanatorium director and a famous Indian cricketer, was replaced in my heart. It was at Orphanides that I met my first wife, Diane. True to form, I immediately fell in love with her.

Diane and her mother had just arrived from Alexandria. At this time I was in Athens on a holiday break from my job as cook and general watchdog on Francis Turville-Petre's island of Aghios Nikolaos, to which I would be returning on the following day.

Cooking for the workmen on the island was not a very complicated job. The chauffeur, Mitso Makri, Francis's trusted right-hand man, was in charge of the commissariat. His instructions were that everything pertaining to the feeding of the workmen should be bought from the village of Khalia, which was home to all the workmen. When essential stocks of groceries were not available in the village, they were bought in the nearest large town, Khalkis, to which weekly or fortnightly visits were made in the island's motor-driven caique.

The rations for the workers, which had been established in their working contracts, hardly allowed me much variation in the menus for three meals a day. One of these might be Indian tea, simmered until black in a large saucepan of water, and sweetened with much sugar, to which each man might add one crushed seed of coriander and the juice of half a lemon. Then, dunking chunks of his daily kilogram loaf, each would consume a third of his bread ration at this simple collation. This strange way with tea seemed to amount to an addiction, for I have never met with it anywhere else in Greece where endless small cups of Turkish coffee have always been the national beverage.

Most of the villagers in Khalia ate meat only once a week, although the island ration was generous. In addition to the habitual *yahni* (stew: see pages 133–140), usually made with kid, there was an allowance of 'butcher's meat', such as a large shoulder of mutton or lamb. This was chopped into chunks of meat, bone and fat, brushed with olive oil, lemon, salt and pepper, then skewered and cooked over a charcoal grill. All the same, the men were perpetually hungry, and I was always dispensing onions to them, which they skinned and ate like oranges, between mouthfuls of bread. Fresh fish from the waters around the island, they either ate fried or skewered and grilled whole over charcoal or as soup (see *Kakavia*, page 35). Pulses, such as beans and lentils, about which I soon learnt a lot, played a vital role in their diet.

In Athens, both Diane and her mother, Molly, expressed a strong wish to visit the island; they had already heard of it in Alexandria. I immediately said that I was sure Francis would be very glad to welcome them, and that perhaps they could stay a week or two. I was delighted with the idea of a prolonged and idyllic courtship on the island.

Not for the first time, I had overstayed, by several months, my *permis de séjour*, and I was due to appear in the Aliens Department to explain myself. I would therefore have to return to Athens in about ten days' time; when I had settled this matter, I would be able to accompany Diane and her mother back to the island and introduce them to their host. I had gravely misjudged the seriousness with which the Aliens Department would take my continued unauthorized presence in the country. I was told quite firmly that, as this was the third time I had misbehaved in this way, they would like me – they pronounced this very firmly – to leave the country in the next two weeks. This meant that not only would I have to say farewell to Francis and the island but I would also have to forgo the pleasures of my planned courtship.

However, in Greece, things are never quite as definite as all that. Even under sentence of death one can expect a reprieve at the very last moment. My news, which put Diane and me into a fairly deep state of gloom, did not seem to worry Francis very much. 'They can't mean it,' he said. 'I'll see Burberry and Walker at the British legation.' And an appointment for me to plead my case at a small bureau of the Greek Foreign Office in Constitution Square was arranged.

Diane and her mother spent a blissful week on the island, fishing, swimming and eating well, and I pressed ahead with my courtship. By the time we left for Athens again, for me to make my appeal, I found that I was engaged to be married.

At the last moment, Diane's mother suggested that we would need a competent interpreter. Consequently, Diane and I were accompanied to the Foreign Office by a certain Kyria Eftychia. Dragon, factotum, interpreter, housekeeper and cook, she had been picked up by Diane's mother in the course of their travels.

During the time she had been thus employed, Kyria Eftychia had grown very attached to my bride-to-be and her mother, and had adopted them to a certain extent. The news of my engagement to Diane sent her into paroxysms of joy, and she readily extended her loyalty to include me. A small attractive woman, about thirty-five years old, she wore widow's weeds, but her extreme liveliness of manner and her keen interest in our romance suggested that she had no intention of remaining in the widowed state. Her reaction, on hearing of my problem with the authorities, was exactly the same as Francis's: a refusal to accept the situation. 'They can't do it! They can't do it! No Greek can turn you out of the country when you are betrothed . . . and just about to be married.'

Accompanied by Diane and Kyria Eftychia, I entered the room to which I had been directed in the Foreign Office, where I was met by an extremely elegant young man who spoke English beautifully. Also in the room were two extremely fashionably dressed young ladies.

The young man introduced himself. 'I am Mr Vrademas. I understand you have come to complain that we are throwing you out.'

'No,' I said. 'I am not coming to complain. You have been most patient, and I have been extremely stupid. I have come to appeal to you. Circumstances have arisen which make it extremely important for me to remain at least a few weeks longer in the country.' At this, I took Diane's hand and brought her across to Mr Vrademas. 'This is my fiancée.'

At once his face burst into smiles. He crossed the room, took the hand of one of the two decorative young ladies, and brought her forward. 'And this is mine,' he said.

These courtesies were scarcely concluded before Vrademas was saying, 'But what a happy conjunction of circumstances!' whereupon he was suddenly assaulted with a flow of speech from Kyria Eftychia, who had crept up behind me.

Vrademas took this address in good part. Although I could not understand all the Kyria said, I gathered that Diane and I were both close friends of the King and Queen of England and that we were direct descendants of Byron, Admiral Lord Codrington and Mr Gladstone. When Kyria Eftychia's flow dried up, Vrademas turned to me and asked, 'When are you getting married?'

I replied that I hoped to arrange it for the following week at the British consulate.

'And where do you intend to spend the honeymoon?'

I said that I had as yet no idea.

'Well,' he said, 'we will give you another six months, and what is more, we will provide a home for your honeymoon. My fiancée's family has a house we hardly ever go to, but it is quite nice. It is on the slopes of Penteli, at a village called Boyati, and it is known as the *spiti Solomou** because it is where Solomos, one of our great poets, used to live and write.'

Vrademas said that he would telephone to get the caretaker to open up the house and see that certain essential services were laid on. Thanking him profusely for his generosity, we hurried home to give the good news to Diane's mother. We decided to go next day to look at the house.

Spiti Solomou turned out to be a charming retreat. Curiously Scottish in flavour, it had a small crenellated tower which contained a library. Two very broad avenues, edged with very tall cypresses, led to it.

Before we settled into our honeymoon home, there had to be a marriage. This took place at the British vice-consulate in Athens and was conducted by Consul Ezard.

The wedding feast which followed was extremely simple, consisting of an enormous saffron pilaf adorned with every kind of delicacy available to the cooks of the chic restaurant, Costi's. However, Kyria Eftychia, who was a witness at the wedding, was as cross as two sticks to find that she was not in charge of the catering

---

* the Solomos house

arrangements. She took her revenge by concocting a number of delicious little filo pastries.

Our arrival at Boyati was by bus, with a mass of impedimenta, and our entry into *spiti Solomou* was a state occasion. A small procession of villagers accompanied us to the front door, and insisted on seeing everything, from the bride and the *yiayia* (my mother-in-law, not too pleased at being described as a grandmother) to the nuptial bed. When curiosity had been satisfied, I accompanied the peasants back to the village and had a few drinks with some older men. Plied mercilessly with resinated wine, I returned to the house pretty well reeling.

Spiti Solomou was an idyllic setting for a honeymoon. For the first few weeks, we spent most of our mornings in bed and the rest of the day taking gentle walks in the neighbourhood and eating the marvellous food that Kyria Eftychia concocted for us. Bread was baked daily in the village, and everyone used the baker's oven for the Sunday feast and for other dishes. Kyria Eftychia made herself familiar with all the facilities, and arranged for supplies of meat, vegetables and so on.

From the castellated tower which contained the 'library' (consisting of a dozen bound volumes of the *Graphic* and the *Illustrated London News*), we could look directly at the great quarry of Pentelic marble which had supplied the material for the Acropolis and the pavement outside Orphanides. Extending for some miles behind the house was a forest of dwarf conifers which it was a great pleasure to explore on our afternoon strolls.

However a radical change was suddenly instituted in our honeymoon routine. This was a result of a hint to Diane from her mother, Molly, to the effect that 'Your father never bothered me much like that.' From the following day, we started to spring up early and try to find something to do to help Kyria Eftychia. Both of us felt an urge to play house and were eager to take part in the domestic chores, especially the cooking. However, Kyria Eftychia insisted on maintaining total control of everything. Our walks now extended from after breakfast until lunch, and from after lunch till dusk when we would return for supper.

I began to wonder if so much walking might turn into a bore. There is, after all, a limit to the time one can spend gazing at unquarried marble.

We devised another way of entertaining ourselves. Both being avid readers, we soon absorbed the comparative history expounded pictorially in the *Graphic* and *Illustrated London News* annuals. Although the main subject of these volumes was the British Empire, with all its heroisms and vicissitudes, much could also be learnt of the more recent history of Eastern Europe, its assassinations and Balkan wars. Certainly, from this reading, we both became authorities on the last years of Queen Victoria's reign and the whole reign and demise of King Edward VII. I was delighted to find a detailed and fully illustrated account of the splendid durbar held by the Viceroy in India to celebrate the coronation of the King and Emperor George V in the year of my birth – 1911.

However, all good things come to an end, and one day both Diane and I found ourselves reading the advertisements for Dr Collis Brown's Chlorodyne, Glauber's Salts and other patent medicines. Suddenly I said, 'I've got an idea. What we need is a new hobby. Something connected with our walks in the forest.'

'Such as what?' Diane asked.

'Tortoises,' I said.

There was a story I had first heard from Leonard Bower, most romantic of Hellenophiles, and as fanatical an admirer of Byron as the Greeks themselves are. Somewhere he had read – he couldn't remember exactly where – that Byron, in his first days in Attica, had looked for and found and marked with his initials, any specially fine specimens of that charming breed, in the hope that at some future date, they might be caught and recognized as having been his. 'But,' Leonard had asserted, 'it was not only Byron who indulged in these shell-signing sessions. Any number of other poets, writers and travellers of fame engaged in the same practice.' Knowing nothing of the longevity of tortoises, he had added, 'Of course it's unlikely that anyone nowadays would find one with Byron's signature on it.'

In his own earlier rambles round Attica, Leonard had himself signed a few tortoises. Perhaps I might find one with *his* name on it.

At first Diane did not fully share my enthusiasm for this new project, and when Molly heard of it, she showed her disapproval by staying in bed for the day. And who should wonder? She had most generously agreed to finance this idyll, but hoped that it would not last too long. Her opinion was that I should now be out trying to find a teaching job. After all, did I not have an Oxford degree? There must be many schools in need of my services as a lecturer on French literature.

Often, during previous walks in the woods, Diane and I had just managed to avoid treading on handsome tortoises. Diane's enthusiasm grew as our hunting proceeded. We would select and bring home only the largest and finest specimens, those with very well-marked shells.

Just outside the *spiti Solomou* we built a strongly protected corral for our captive pets, one wall of the house forming its rear boundary. Inspection of the new arrivals was carried out with minute care and we always made sure that plenty of green stuff of all kinds was scattered round their quarters.

Kyria Eftychia took against them from the moment the first three had been brought home in triumph. Superficially her objection was practical. *'Den einai fagi.'* ('They're not food.') – though she had heard that some Albanian Turks made a soup out of them. 'Perish the thought!' I said. It suddenly became clear to me that Eftychia was jealous of our new-found pets. This jealousy worked in my favour, for she began to invite me into her kitchen.

Like many superb cooks, she tended to conceal her mysteries, if she could. Now, however, she would come out and interrupt our tortoise races with the words, 'Kyrie Yiorgo, I am making *dolmades* for tonight' or 'I have a marvellous octopus. Come and see.' (Kyria Eftychia's Octopus stew is on page 56.)

I was fascinated to observe Eftychia's skill and it was at this time when I was being made more free of the kitchen, that I first noticed the presence of 'followers', as the Victorians used to say.

There was one who seemed to make a daily appearance: Tsoukalas (literally, 'saucepan maker'). Eftychia introduced him as a brilliant young lawyer with political connections. At the same time I was aware that some kind of passion – albeit suppressed – was seething in the kitchen. This confirmed my earlier impression that Eftychia had no intention of remaining single.

The day came when Diane, who had also been aware of tension in the atmosphere, informed me that something was going on in her mother's bedroom. Kyria Eftychia was in there with a gentleman, and they seemed to be conspiring about something; every time she went in, their voices became hushed. However, it was not long before Molly came out with the whole story. The conspiracy was a benign one, its object being to get me employed.

If – Molly said – I would only play my cards right, I could, with a very small investment, became the owner of a national weekly newspaper. After getting an explanation from Eftychia, I was able to relate the whole story to Diane. It was a typical Greek political imbroglio.

When the anti-royalist President Venizelos had fallen from power and the Royalists had taken over, all the various Venizelist publications had been suppressed. Among them an important one was *I Dimokratiki Drasis (Democratic Action)*. This had been a national and very well respected paper. By fortunate chance, its actual title and important printing blocks which gave it its character were now available for a reasonable sum of money. So was a brilliant pro-Venizelist editor. The moment the title was bought, the paper could appear again. The sum involved, according to Eftychia, was only fifty pounds. If I were willing, Molly would be glad to produce that sum to make me the owner.

I cannot really blame myself, nor can I blame Molly who was naturally optimistic, being a devoted Christian Scientist. She thought that my unemployment problem could be solved by this modest expenditure. What she did not understand was that it was absolutely illegal for any foreigner to own a newspaper in Greece and that, in following Tsoukalas and Eftychia's advice, she was, in effect, arranging for us all to be kicked out. I too was ignorant of this, though I demurred a little at the whole scheme. However, when Molly asked me if I would at least go down to Athens and see the prospective editor, I agreed.

Eleftherios Eleftherodopoulos was an absolutely charming and obviously brilliant young man. On the question of a foreigner owning a Greek newspaper, he said that what was at issue was not the ownership but the money that was needed to purchase the title.

Two days later I went down to Athens again, met some other members of the once and future staff, and became the owner, personally, of the paper's title.

After this, I spent some time with a Captain Alexander Desipris (Royal Hellenic Navy) whom the editor had appointed Economic Director. Various documents had been prepared, in duplicate, and I signed one set, and he the other. Desipris and the editor then congratulated me.

I returned to Boyati on the bus, to be greeted by Eftychia and by Molly as a conquering hero. I admitted that I could not remember the question of remuneration for me having been raised during my conversations in Athens. However, Eftychia found a paragraph in the papers Desipris and I had signed which undertook to pay me twenty per cent of the profits, when the newspaper had established itself.

One thing that the editor had made extremely clear to me was that my presence would not be required at the newspaper's offices during the coming three or four weeks which would be required for preparation of the first three issues of the paper. When these three issues were ready, the proofs would be left with blank spaces where late news of political and social events could be inserted. I would be able to check the contents with a lawyer of high standing, who would see that no libellous or obscene material was included.

As far as Eftychia was concerned, I was now 'Golden Boy'. All my arrangements had been so skilfully carried through, showing that I was indeed a business man, and that, in a very short time, we should all be rich. She was, however, pained that I had come back from Athens without any arrangement having been made for her friend Tsoukalas to receive a commission for introducing these wealthy English backers. (I heard later, from Diane, that her mother had added ten pounds for this commission to her £50 investment.)

If I had any misgivings about the transactions into which I had so light-heartedly entered, I did not pass these on to Diane. She had meanwhile developed a strong affection for our tortoise pets. Indeed, during my short absence in Athens she had gathered together some four or five brilliantly marked specimens of especial splendour.

As I grew in Kyria Eftychia's favour and esteem, so were any doubts allayed in Diane's mind. Her mother's fears could not so easily be set at rest. In advancing the money towards the buying of the newspaper, her first idea had been to find me immediate employment, remove me from the pernicious habit of collecting tortoises and, in the course of time, make a good profit on her investment. But here I was, still playing with tortoises, I had no job which would enable me to commute to Athens daily, and it would be many months before she could hope to see any return on her investment. At the same time, she was seeing less and less of Eftychia, who showed every sign of forming a permanent connection with Tsoukalas.

Meanwhile, Eftychia had obviously begun to brood on the condition of my soul. Molly had long ago made her a keen convert to Christian Science, and I was awarded the supreme accolade when she placed under my pillow a copy of Mary Baker Eddy's *Science and Health*.

Our collection of tortoises grew apace, but though we had specimens of all kinds, on none had we been able to find markings which might be construed as those of poets or, indeed, of any other human being. To prevent them escaping – at which they were extremely skilled – we had to reinforce the stone walls of their corral several times. One day I was in the kitchen, watching Kyria Eftychia cook. She was now on good terms with the tortoises to the extent that she had given up pointing two fingers to avert the evil eye whenever she passed them. 'Can tortoises sing?' I asked her.

'Of course not,' she replied. 'Singing tortoises, indeed!' She looked at me curiously. Perhaps she was wondering if Mary Baker Eddy was beginning to affect me.

That night, both Diane and I woke up at about eleven o'clock. There was a sound of stones being knocked together. Diane joined me at the window from which one could look straight down into our corral of tortoises. Soon we were joined by Eftychia, clad in her widow's nightwear and looking like Lady Macbeth.

'It's the *Kalikantzari*,' she said, 'but this is not the time of year for them.' (*Kalikantzari* are gnome-like creatures who come to earth on Christmas Eve for twelve days. They clatter about on the roofs, and do all sorts of damage.)

The knocking suddenly stopped, and then the strange music began. To give Eftychia the lie, the tortoises were singing.

Molly was now awake, and joined us. 'Those filthy animals!' she exclaimed. 'They'll be breaking into the house next.'

Diane said, 'You know, George, I don't think they're happy here. Let's liberate them.'

So we did, while Eftychia stayed for about an hour with Molly, before retreating downstairs to her little room off the kitchen.

The tortoises made no particular speed as we pulled down the stone walls, but when we got up next morning, there were only one or two laggards in sight, some distance away from the house, moving towards the forest.

Perhaps the tortoises' spontaneous orgy had been an omen. For that very morning Tsoukalas appeared with a message that I was wanted at the newspaper offices. Something had come up which made it necessary to bring forward the launch date of the paper's first issue. The proofs were ready for me. The lawyer awaited me and

I should appear at the office as soon as I could.

I was given a sheaf of proofs – with spaces in them where the editor could insert late items of news. I was conducted to the lawyer's office, where we sat down and began to peruse the proofs. There was nothing in what I read that could justify my vetoing it. Where I could not understand, the lawyer, Sophoulis, explained to me in rather bad English.

By this time, I myself had become excited about the project and, on my returning to the office, Eleftherios asked me if I would like to watch the printing of the paper and see it come off the press. Nothing could have delighted me more. He told me the printer's address and what time to be there. I was young and stupid. The idea of seeing the birth of a paper which was in a sense 'mine' thrilled me.

I seem to remember that at this time all newspapers in Athens were printed on the same press. At the printer's, I was interested to see that the local communist paper – still allowed to be printed – was emerging on a printing bed next to that from which ours would come surging out.

With the editor's arrival at the printer, certain small additions were made to the paper's content. I was not aware what these consisted of. I only remember the glorious moment when the paper came off the press, the ink wet on it, and was put into bundles and taken away to be distributed.

Eleftherios led the way to an enormous café in Omonia where many people always gathered to drink coffee and read the papers. We sat down to await the appearance of ours. This was one of the great moments of my life, idiotic though the whole project was.

Suddenly the newsvendors seemed to fill the square. They ran from café to café, distributing the papers to all and sundry. As they approached us, Eleftherios snatched two or three copies for himself, and two for me. At this very moment, the square was flooded with policemen who went around, snatching copies of the paper from the hands of all those who had bought them.

'Hey!' I said as my copies were roughly snatched from my hands.

'Fascist pigs!' said Eleftherios. He had managed to sit on two of his copies, and when the force of policemen dispersed, he gave me one, saying, 'I don't know what's gone wrong, but we'll talk about it tomorrow.'

However, as far as the newspaper was concerned, there was to be no tomorrow.

With my copy of the newspaper scrunched up in my pocket, I took the bus back to *spiti Solomou*. Appearing at the front door, I felt like the ghost of Banquo. Pulling the paper out of my pocket, I handed it to Eftychia, who was in the kitchen. If Tsoukalas had been there, I would probably have hit him. She opened the paper and looked at it with pride. 'At last!' she said. 'Here it is!'

'Read it,' I said. It was difficult for me to read Greek, and therefore to find whatever it was that could possibly have caused the intervention by the police.

'What is wrong with it?' she asked. 'It is magnificent. Congratulations. It is a marvellous paper. It always was.'

Looking through it myself, it was about two hours before I found the blemish. One of the blank spaces had been filled in with a minute and detailed history of the medico-sexual problems of the Greek royal family. It spared no one: man, woman or child. This, I thought, must be the work of a saboteur. I would go to see Eleftherios next day, and we would track down the person responsible.

Diane accepted the debacle with remarkable equanimity. In fact she thought it was an enormous joke. She attached no blame to me, but said that someone would have to tell her mother what had happened.

'Not me, I hope,' I said.

'No, I'll tell her,' Diane said, and went upstairs at once.

Molly took the news remarkably well. 'At least these Greeks are entertaining,' she said.

Although I was glad that Molly and Diane were so light-hearted, I did not feel the same. I sensed the danger of a case of criminal libel against the owners of the paper. Although I believed that my name had not yet been officially registered as owner, it would not take the police long to discover my purchase of the title.

Eleftherios would be in very serious danger. I took the earliest bus to Athens next morning, and went straight to the newspaper offices. He was there. He was profuse in his apologies to me. He could not imagine how it had happened. Substitution at the printing works was the only possible explanation ... probably the work of a communist.

As we sat drinking our mandatory small coffees, I could not help admiring the way Eleftherios was taking this whole disaster, for he was now facing the probability of a long term in prison. As for me, he said I did not have to worry. 'Just go back to the village, and stay there quietly. With any luck, it will be a long time before they discover you're involved at all. I'm sure Desipris hasn't been efficient enough to register your name. But get out of Athens now. I'll let you know through my lawyer where I am. This is the one place you should not be found . . . and talking to me.'

There was a noise from downstairs. A minute or two later, Desipris appeared in the doorway accompanied by two policemen. Making myself small, I managed to squeeze between the policemen, and downstairs. I hurried to the bus stop to catch the next bus to Boyati.

Back at *spiti Solomou*, an atmosphere of euphoria persisted. It was not until Molly began to understand the meanings of various medical phrases in the article that she started to suspect that her investment was entirely lost.

Meanwhile, Eleftherios was in jail, awaiting trial, and Desipris was in a naval lock-up of some kind. But we remained, for the moment, undisturbed by the police.

In the fourth week, Tsoukalas arrived at *spiti Solomou*, and reported that Eleftherios was being sent into exile. On the day appointed for his departure, I went to Piraeus, taking him some cigarettes. We have never met since, but I heard that he had founded a Greek-language newspaper in America and was extremely successful.

There was less dignity about our own departure from Greece shortly after. This involved a painful meeting with our benefactor, Vrademas, who had so graciously overlooked my earlier misdemeanours . . . and lent us *spiti Solomou*. After fond farewells to Eftychia, with whom Molly kept in touch for many years, we sailed. It took a war to bring me back again.

*   *   *

I was in the Middle East from 1940 until 1946. While, in its later stages, in Cairo and in Istanbul, 'my war' held gastronomic excitements, it did not begin well. As a military policeman in Egypt and then in Cyprus, I lacked opportunities to sample the local fleshpots. Indeed my chief Cyprus memories of those days are of the bugs in Wolseley Barracks in Nicosia and of a savage bout of sandfly fever that landed me in hospital. (All the local insects were evidently strongly attracted to me.)

Then the Division moved from Cyprus to Iraq. In Haifa, *en route*, we were surprised when the citizens gave us a rousing welcome, whole-heartedly supported by the local Press. This bolstered the general morale of troops and particularly of us military police, or 'red caps' – never the most popular of men in any area. It was gratifying to see, boldly displayed in the local paper, a notice to the effect that all members of the British Forces had been granted temporary membership of the Sodom and Gomorrah Golf Club. The fact that I would only be in Haifa for a few days did not diminish the glamour of this offer.

We were not so popular with the citizens of Baghdad, and as we led the line of march out of the city, on our way to Kirkuk, we suddenly had the experience, in a large and teeming market place, of being stoned. This attempt at a Biblical execution was not very serious, the missiles being, for the most part, pebbles, hurled at us by crowds of children, urged on by their malevolent mothers. Dogs of all shapes and sizes were being set to snap at our legs in an attempt to unbalance us from our motor-bikes, but they lost the battle against our sturdy boots.

One day, camped on the western side of Kirkuk, a couple of senior NCOs returned to the camp on their motor-bikes, bearing with them an extraordinary bottle of some peculiar colourless liquid. This carried no proprietary mark on its label, only the rough image of an old-fashioned biplane, presumably to indicate that the content was a pretty high flier. I tasted this liquid immediately, was stricken with horror by the taste of it, and was choking when the bottle was snatched from my hand. Before I could stop them, my companions had all imbibed the equivalent of a good small cupful to each man. I was instantly faced by a tent filled with a raging mob of drunks.

Luckily I had just prepared for them a very powerful curry of bully beef and tinned sausages, and this proved helpful in reducing their hysteria.

A day later, John Lepper, a senior NCO, and I went out looking for a small café which was said to be buried in the sand, and to be authorized for use by troops. We sighted a light some hundred yards off, and then both John and I were struck with awe to recognize the sound of Bach's 3rd Brandenburg Concerto emerging out of the sand from which this rudimentary tavern had been dug.

The menu we were offered did not, in any way, match the grandeur of the overture. The proprietor of this establishment, who turned out to be an Assyrian, was obviously proud of it. He welcomed us warmly and displayed the delicacies he had available. There was a choice of three tins: one of baked beans, one of bully beef and one of pilchards. Lepper and I opted for pilchards and beans. Our *maître d'hotel* started, with some ceremony, to open the tins, saying, 'These are very fresh. You see – no dents! Open now, for you only. Very fresh!'

It was indeed a far cry from such repasts to the feasts I enjoyed, after I had been commissioned in Cairo, as a result of the hospitality of Elizabeth David. As I have described elsewhere, she introduced me to a fresh world of culinary delights, the world she would also introduce to thousands of ration-weary, taste-starved Britons when *A Book of Mediterranean Food* was first published in 1950.

From Cairo I was posted to the British Embassy in Istanbul for a year, and there I was able to explore Turkish cuisine in some depth. Later, my efforts to wangle a posting to Greece were successful, and I remained there until I returned to England at the end of 1946.

*   *   *

I was not to be in the Middle East again until 1974, when I visited Cyprus with my soon-to-be-wife, Caroline. Her mother, the late Milla Cavendish, and her sister, Anne, offered us the most lavish hospitality in their house in Limassol and all over the island. I was now able to appreciate Cyprus in a way I had certainly not been able to in 1940.

It was in 1978 that, recklessly deciding we could support ourselves by our writings, Caroline and I came to live in Cyprus. Now, at the age of eighty, I have spent over twelve years on this delightful island. In gastronomic terms, even though – or perhaps because? – I lack the voracious appetite of youth, this has been a fruitful period.

Cyprus is now a polyglot home for people from all over the Middle East, and most especially for thousands who have had to escape from war-racked Beirut, always famed for its sybaritic yet subtle cuisine. As a result I have been able to enlarge and deepen my previously sketchy knowledge of Arab cookery. Apart from the treats I enjoyed with Elizabeth David, most of the food I ate in

Egypt was the very 'frenchified' cuisine of hotels and restaurants. It is only recently that I have explored the more down-to-earth dishes to whose re-discovery Egyptian nationalism has led.

I have also found another source of great culinary interest: the secret cuisine of Cyprus. I say 'secret' because you will not encounter it in hotels and tourist restaurants. Only in private houses and those (usually modest) eating-places which maintain traditional country cookery will you discover this.

Greece has always had one foot in the West and the other in the East. Cyprus definitely belongs to the Middle East. When I refer to Cypriot friends of mine, in this book, I invariably mean Greek Cypriots. This is because, since the Turkish invasion of 1974, Turkish Cypriots live in an occupied zone to which I do not have access. (As a foreigner, I might be allowed over the 'Green Line' on day trips, but since the Greek Cypriots amongst whom I live cannot cross that frontier, I am unwilling to do so.)

I hope whole-heartedly that this situation may change. However, speaking in terms of cookery, I must make the point that the traditional Cypriot cuisine I describe here is that of both the communities who formerly shared the island peacefully. You can call it Greco-Turkish or Turko-Greek: both those terms mean what I call 'Cypriot'. I have found that this has a great deal to offer to the gastronome and, of course, the cook.

MEZÉ

N O ONE SEEMS to know the origins of the word 'mezé', though many suggestions, ranging from the Persian word for 'table' to the Italian *mezzano* (meaning 'middle', which makes no sense at all), have been put forward. Various peoples of the Middle East – Greek, Arab, Turkish – regard it (differently spelt) as their own. In Greek, it means 'a little delicacy' or a meal made up of such delicacies. I shall use it in both these senses. (The accent is an aid to pronunciation.)

In some Middle Eastern countries, you will be offered a 'full' mezé, including many dishes which I describe elsewhere in this book: cooked vegetables, salads, grains and pulses, little sausages and rissoles, kebabs, even stews. But few people serve a meal of this kind at home often. In Cyprus it is usually referred to as a 'taverna mezé'. In some Cypriot restaurants in London, you will find, at a set price, a 'full mezé' for four people, which will traditionally include a bottle of Cyprus brandy. We have found that a 'full taverna mezé' is a real treat for young hungry visitors, though nowadays the thought of its endless courses makes me, personally, flinch.

In contrast, a mezé can consist merely of a saucer of olives or nuts, or strips of cucumber in a glass of salted water. Such a (free) accompaniment to drinks used to be invariable in Greece, Turkey and Cyprus. Recently, the drinking habits of tourists – especially the British – have led to its being often omitted, but no indigenous person drinks alcohol without eating something.

Various kinds of small mezé are ideal for civilised drinks parties.

With the addition of vegetable dishes, and perhaps one substantial one, such as *Moussaka* (page 140), mezé can provide a delicious summer buffet.

Mezé has been translated by some people as *hors d'oeuvres*, and many of the recipes I give here make ideal first courses, served with Arab or pitta bread, or indeed any good fresh crusty loaf. However I also see these 'mezés' as providing nutritious and delicious meals, very much in keeping with two trends. First, the tendency to eat 'on the hoof' (that is, not sitting down at the table for a set meal), and secondly, the movement towards a meat-free diet.

Elsewhere in this book I have given various croquettes which can be included under the heading of 'mezé', and at the end of this chapter one or two small snacks which belong nowhere else are described. However my main concentration is on what I feel compelled to call 'dips'.

I say 'compelled' because the word has terrible associations for me, bringing to mind concoctions of powdered onion soup and sour cream which used to be handed round with potato crisps which invariably broke when one attempted to use them to scoop up the (un)savoury mixture. I assure you that the 'dips' that follow are quite different. Some people call them 'salads', as with *taramosalata*, but they are not salads in any British sense. I suppose they could be described as 'sauces' but though I have been known to use *tahini* or even *taramosalata* in this way in restaurants, as an alternative to olive oil and lemon, with grilled fish, this is not their purpose. They are intended to be eaten with bread dipped into them (or spread with them, if you insist). With good bread and a salad, they are indeed . . . a meal.

Hummus bi-tahina

Hummus with tahini
Egypt (and elsewhere)

This dip of chick peas with tahini is popular throughout the Arab world and in Britain. I advise against buying it ready-made and tinned, though you can make it with tinned chick peas.

250 g/8 oz cooked chick peas
the juice of 1 to 2 lemons
150 ml/¼ pint tahini
2 to 3 cloves of garlic, crushed

garnish:
1 tablespoon finely chopped
　parsley
1 tablespoon olive oil, mixed
　with ½ teaspoon paprika
a few of the cooked chick peas

If you are not using tinned chick peas, prepare and cook them as on page 35, reserving a few for garnish. Mash the chick peas or use the metal blade of the food processor – in this case putting in the lemon juice first. Add the other ingredients. The result should be a thick, slightly grainy purée. Season with salt to taste. Leave to cool. Then garnish with a trickle of oil and paprika, a scattering, or pattern, of chick peas and the parsley.

Variations: Indefatigable lemonizers may squeeze on extra lemon juice at the table.
As in Tahinosalata (page 159) many Cypriots add 4 tablespoons of olive oil to the mixture.

Baba Ghanoush

Lebanon

This aubergine and tahina dip has a rich, smoky taste that is peculiarly beguiling ... almost addictive.

450 g/1 lb aubergines
2 to 3 cloves of garlic, crushed
　with 1 teaspoon salt
150 ml/¼ pint tahini
150 ml/¼ pint lemon juice

garnish:
1 tablespoon olive oil
1 tablespoon parsley

Make one or two slits in the aubergines. Then, ideally, grill them over an open flame until the skins are blackened and blistered and the flesh soft. You can achieve a similar result by roasting them in a very hot oven or putting them under the grill. Leave to cool. Then cut off the ends and peel off the skins. Squeeze the flesh to get rid of excess moisture. Now either mash the flesh with the crushed garlic, or – as I do – purée it in the food processor. Add the tahini and lemon juice gradually, tasting as you go till the seasoning suits you – and you may want to add more salt and some freshly ground black pepper. Put the mixture on a flat serving dish, and garnish with the olive oil and parsley.

Variation: Some people add ½ teaspoon cumin to the mixture.

Avocado with tahini

Cyprus

Avocados are now being grown most successfully in Cyprus, and acquire a Middle Eastern quality in the following (non-traditional) recipe for a small rich dip.

2 ripe avocados, peeled and pitted	1 tablespoon cold water
1 clove of garlic, crushed with ½ teaspoon salt	3 tablespoons parsley, very finely chopped
4 tablespoons lemon juice	a pinch of cumin
1 tablespoon tahini	salt and freshly ground black pepper

Mash the avocado flesh with the garlic and half the lemon juice. Beat up the tahini with the rest of the lemon juice and the cold water. (The small quantity of tahini prevents the flavour of the avocado being swamped.) Combine all ingredients. Taste and season.

Salata jazar

Carrot dip
Egypt

Here is a joy for all cumin lovers. (By the way, why have people started pronouncing this *kew*min? Please pronounce it correctly, as in 'Comin' through the Rye'.) This dip can be prepared very quickly.

450 g/1 lb carrots, cooked
     until tender and drained*
4 tablespoons olive oil
2 tablespoons lemon juice
2 teaspoons cumin
3 cloves of garlic, crushed

1 teaspoon salt
½ teaspoon cayenne pepper

garnish:
a scattering of parsley, finely
     chopped

Mash all the ingredients or purée them in a blender or food processor. Chill and garnish with parsley.

Fava

Lentil dip
Greece

450 g/1 lb yellow lentils
1 large onion, chopped
150 ml/¼ pint olive oil
salt and freshly ground black
     pepper

garnish:
a small jug of olive oil
a small onion, finely chopped
a sprinkle of parsley, finely
     chopped

Wash the lentils, cover with water and bring to the boil. Remove any scum that rises to the surface. Now add the onion and oil, and cook until soft. Add the salt and pepper. Drain off any excess water, and mash or purée in a food processor. Serve in a bowl – sprinkled with parsley, if you like – with crusty bread, chopped onion and olive oil.

Ful nabed

Broad bean dip
Egypt

Ful nabed is the name of the dried broad beans which you can buy from most Middle Eastern shops. Buy the skinless ones. The others need hours of soaking, and you have to remove the skins.

---

* I keep tinned carrots in my store cupboard solely to make this dip in minutes. The texture is perfect, and the garlic and spices ensure no problem with flavour. You must, of course, drain the carrots.

250g/8 oz dried broad beans
  (preferably skinned)
2 medium onions, finely
  chopped
75 ml/3 fl oz olive oil
salt and freshly ground black
  pepper

2 tablespoons lemon juice
½ teaspoon mint

garnish:
2 tablespoons olive oil
a pinch of paprika
2 teaspoons parsley, chopped

To be on the safe side, soak even these skinless beans for several hours and drain.

Fry the onions in the olive oil till they are soft and just taking colour. Add 500 ml/18 fl oz of water and bring to the boil. Put in the drained beans and simmer, without salt, for 2 hours or more, until the beans are really soft. There should be hardly any liquid left. You may have to add a little more water during cooking, if the beans are not soft enough. Mash them, or put them in the food processor with salt and black pepper to taste, the lemon juice and mint. The result should be a thick purée ... almost a paste.

To garnish pour the oil on top, and sprinkle with paprika and parsley. Serve with bread and lemon wedges.

Red lentil dip

This is not a traditional recipe, but my wife invented it in Cyprus and its ingredients make it very Middle Eastern.

250 g/8 oz red lentils
1 medium onion, chopped
2 cloves of garlic, crushed with
  1 teaspoon salt
1 medium onion, grated
100 ml/4 fl oz olive oil
2 teaspoons cumin

salt and freshly ground black
  pepper

garnish:
a sprinkling of olive oil
a scattering of parsley, chopped

Thoroughly wash the lentils. Bring to the boil with the chopped onion and the garlic. Skim off any scum and cook until tender, for about 30 minutes. Drain off any excess liquid. Mash, or purée in the food processor, with the grated raw onion, olive oil, cumin and salt and pepper. Chill, garnish and serve.

Taramosalata

Fish-roe dip
Greece and Cyprus

My relationship with this is a complex one. For years, I have been boring people with Athenian memories of *avgotarakho* which is the dried, pressed and smoked eggs of the grey mullet. I used to eat it cut into thin, thin slices outside Orphanides' bar. Today it is almost as expensive, and as hard to obtain, as caviare. It is almost as good too. Smoked cod's roe has to suffice for various recipes.

I am fond of *tarama*, for which you pound 250 g/8 oz smoked cod's roe with the juice of 1 or 2 lemons; then you dribble in 150 ml/¼ pint olive oil, while continuing to pound. This is one of those recipes for which the food processor won't do.

From this bracing mixture, I evolved what I found to be a pleasing version of *taramosalata* . . . so often, nowadays, an insipid concoction, sometimes tinted a most peculiar shade of strawberry.

2 cloves of garlic, crushed and pounded	1 tablespoon freshly ground black pepper
225 g/8 oz smoked cod's roe, skinned	1½ tablespoons olive oil
100 g/4 oz cream cheese	1 tablespoon lemon juice

Mix the garlic, cod's roe and cream cheese together thoroughly, seasoning with pepper. Very gradually work in first the olive oil and then the lemon juice.

I presented this to a beautiful and sensitive visitor . . . and she was shocked by it. To halve the quantity of cod's roe might have helped a little, but what she really wanted was the light, almost fluffy, pink mixture she had tasted in restaurants. Here is my version of this.

4 slices white bread, crusts removed	1 clove garlic, crushed
100 g/4 oz smoked cod's roe, skinned	1 tablespoon onion, pulverized
	6 to 8 tablespoons olive oil
	the juice of 1 lemon

Cover the bread with cold water. Then squeeze dry. Combine with the roe, garlic and onion. Add olive oil and lemon juice alternately a little at a time, whisking the while. If the final mixture is too thick for you, thin very carefully, with a little cold water, added drip by drip.

Some people, though not I, substitute mashed potato for the soaked bread.

Falafel

Chick pea balls
Lebanon

Charles Snow of Nicosia, long resident in the Middle East, is acknowledged by many to be the 'falafel king'. Here is his excellent recipe.

225 g/8 oz chick peas	2 teaspoons coriander powder
2 medium onions	3 to 4 teaspoons cumin
3 cloves of garlic	$\frac{1}{2}$ teaspoon baking powder
3 green chillis (optional)	salt to taste
a handful of parsley, chopped	

Soak the chick peas overnight, drain and grind finely, using the metal blade of a food processor. Grind onions, garlic, chillis and parsley finely and mix thoroughly with the chick peas, together with the coriander, cumin, baking powder and salt. Form into small flattened balls and deep fry in hot oil until the outside is brown. Serve with *Tahiniyeh* (see page 158).

Charles gives two useful addenda: 'The tricky bit is getting the Falafel into a frying basket without breaking them up, and this difficulty can be surmounted with little loss of flavour by freezing them first. Cook from frozen. Secondly, if served as a sandwich inside Arab bread with chopped tomatoes and parsley and tahina sauce (see page 158) poured over, they provide a substantial meal which makes vegetarians purr with delight.'

Note: The word 'falafel' is said to come from 'umm al-falafel', meaning 'mother of peppers'. This seems to encourage the inclusion of the green chillis.

Merjimek koftesi

Lentil balls
Turkey

350 g/12 oz brown lentils
1 large onion, finely chopped
1 tablespoon olive oil
1 large very ripe tomato
salt and freshly ground black
  pepper

2 tablespoons finely chopped
  parsley
1½ teaspoons cumin
350 g/12 oz fine burghul (see
  page 67)

Boil the lentils until very tender. Drain thoroughly. Leave to cool. Fry the onion until soft in the oil. Add to the lentils with the tomato – grated – and the parsley, cumin, salt, pepper and rinsed burghul. Knead all together with your hands so that the juices are thoroughly absorbed into the burghul. Leave to stand for 30 minutes and then roll into little balls.

Elies marinates

Marinated olives
Cyprus

At the market in Limassol we see heaps of fresh green olives, waiting to be cracked, pickled with vine leaves and slices of lemon and then dressed in the following way. Alas, this ritual cannot be observed in Britain, but you can adapt it to the olives you buy in brine.

225 g/8 oz green olives,
  pickled in brine
1 lemon, chopped into small
  pieces

2 cloves of garlic, crushed
2 tablespoons coriander seeds,
  coarsely pounded
3 tablespoons olive oil

Rinse the olives in a colander or sieve. Put them into a bowl with all the other ingredients. Stir well and leave overnight.

CHEESE IN THE MEZÉ

On page 179 I look at cheeses of the Middle East. As you will find, they do not arouse me to great enthusiasm, but I do like them 'dressed up' in the ways they are often presented in a mezé.

Feta ya Mezé

Dressed Feta
Cyprus

175 to 225 g/6 to 8 oz Feta
1 tablespoon fresh mint, finely chopped, or 1 teaspoon dried mint, crumbled

1½ tablespoons olive oil ⎱ well
2 teaspoons lemon juice ⎰ mixed

Cut the cheese into small slices carefully, because it's so crumbly. Set the slices out, overlapping slightly, on a plate. Scatter the mint on top, and pour over the oil and lemon juice. Eat with a fork.

Haloumi psito i tiganito

Grilled or fried Haloumi
Cyprus

I think this slightly rubbery, often mint-flavoured cheese (now widely available in Britain) is at its best grilled or fried.

Grilling: ideally, grill the slices of Haloumi over charcoal, but your electric or gas grill will do. Cut the cheese into slices 1.2 cm/½ inch thick, and grill till they brown and bubble. Serve with wedges of lemon to squeeze over the cheese.

Frying: heat a little olive oil in a small pan. (Before frying, you can dip the cheese in oil, but it isn't necessary.) Fry the slices (1.2 cm/½ inch thick) for about 1 minute on each side. Serve with wedges of lemon to squeeze over it. (Some people squeeze lemon juice over the cheese while it is frying and then dip the bread they eat with the cheese in the lemon-flavoured oil.)

PRESERVED MEATS IN THE MEZÉ

Three delicious preserved meats, all of which should be sliced paper thin, make excellent additions to the mezé:

Aboukht/basturma

Dried beef with fenugreek and garlic
Armenia

Closely related to the Rumanian pastrami, now popular in the United States 'on rye', you will find this electrifying Armenian creation in Cyprus, in Greece, in Egypt, in the Lebanon, and probably in other places too. It is beef, coated with a paste of garlic, fenugreek, chilli pepper and other spices, and dried. It is fiery and flavourful. Slice it as finely as possible and arrange on a plate. (If you fry it, do so very briefly, as it will quickly toughen and acquire a bitter taste.)

In Egypt they eat *basturma* with fried eggs for breakfast.

Hiromeri

Smoked leg of pork
Cyprus

This is a very great delicacy. Indeed, if sliced thinly enough, it seems to me quite the equal of Parma ham and, like Parma ham, it can be enjoyed with melon or fresh figs as a first course, though this is not traditional. The leg of pork is cured in wine and spices and smoked. It is expensive and highly appreciated. Arrange oblong wafers on a plate.

Lounza

Smoked pork fillet
Cyprus

Not quite such a treat – or as expensive – as *hiromeri*, but nonetheless very good, this fillet of pork is spiced, sometimes marinated in wine, and smoked. Slices can be grilled over charcoal, or fried, but it is best simply sliced . . . hardly ever thinly enough for me.

SOUPS

WHEN I THINK of Middle Eastern soups, my mind fills with the delicious aromas of well-seasoned vegetables and spiced pulses, and with the fragrance of lemons.

Most of the soups I describe here are substantial and nourishing: quite as suited to the British climate as to that of their countries of origin. Most of them are, or can be, vegetarian. Often this is simply a question of what stock you use. In most of these soups, this can be meat, chicken or vegetable (sometimes fish).

I give in fact only three soups containing meat. In one case, *Youvarlakia* (see page 32), it takes the delicate form of little savoury meat balls. On the whole I believe that actual pieces of meat belong not in soups but in stews. However there are two famous soups which I feel I really can't ignore.

One is *Mayeritsa*, the traditional Greek Easter soup, eaten on the return from the midnight church service. To those who have been fasting throughout Lent (as many Greeks and Cypriots still do) it is a great treat, and I (though without the benefits, to the appetite and soul, of a fast) have much enjoyed it with friends. The other soup is *Patsia*, usually eaten in very different circumstances, as it is a speciality of late-night restaurants in what, in Limassol, is known as the 'cabaret' district. I have eaten it at the old, alas now defunct, Rose Hotel of Mr and Mrs Triandafillides (the word means 'son of a rose') where it was served with a fiery sauce brought from North Africa. A similar effect could be achieved with Tabasco.

The problem with both these soups is their ingredients, which I fear squeamish British cooks may be unwilling to handle. However, for interest, and in the hope of a more adventurous spirit in what many predict will be the more earthy 'nineties', I offer recipes.

Mayeritsa

Easter soup
Greece and Cyprus

450 g/1 lb lamb's tripe
2 lamb's lungs
1 lamb's heart
1 lamb's liver
the juice of 2 large or 4 small lemons
6 spring onions or 2 medium onions, finely chopped
50 g/2 oz butter
2 teaspoons dill, chopped

1.75 litres/3 pints stock or water
75 g/3 oz long-grain rice, washed
3 eggs
2 tablespoons parsley, finely chopped
salt and freshly ground black pepper

Rinse the tripe and put it in a pan of cold water. Bring to the boil, skim, rinse and drain. Wash the lungs, heart and liver and cover them with water, to which you have added the juice of 1 large or 2 small lemons; leave for 30 minutes. Then bring them to the boil; skim, rinse and drain again. Cut the tripe, lungs, heart and liver into small pieces.

Sauté the onion in the butter until soft. Add the dill and the chopped meats, and stir. Put in a heavy pan, and pour over the stock. Season with salt and pepper. Simmer over very low heat for 2 hours, covered. Add the rice and cook for a further 20 minutes. Finally beat the eggs until frothy, adding the remaining lemon juice and 1 tablespoon of cold water. Slowly add 1 tablespoon of hot stock from the meats, whisking all the time. Add 2 more spoonfuls in the same way. Now incorporate the egg mixture into the body of the stock, whisking constantly. In no circumstances allow to boil, or the eggs will curdle. Sprinkle the parsley over generously.

Patsia

Lamb's head soup
Cyprus

An altogether less lively version of this soup is eaten in Greece. I far
prefer the Cypriot one.

1 lamb's head *or* 1 kg/2¼ lb
lamb soup-bones, 6 lambs'
tongues and 3 sets of lamb's
brains *or* 1 kg/2¼ lb lamb
soup bones and 6 sets of
lamb's brains
vinegar
1 medium onion, whole
1 carrot, whole
1 celery stick, whole
2 ripe medium tomatoes,
roughly chopped

2 cloves garlic, whole
4 bay leaves
salt and freshly ground black
pepper

garnish:
slices of fried bread, 1 per
person
garlic cloves crushed to a purée
with equal parts of wine
vinegar and lemon juice *or* a
pepper sauce such as Tabasco

You can make an excellent soup just using the bones and the brains,
fresh or frozen, and that is what I suggest, as the traditional main
ingredient can be off-putting. You will have to clean the lamb's head
and cut it in half before boiling it, skimming for a long time. If you
use the tongues, you will have to scrape and prepare them, putting
them with the stew bones in cold water, simmering and skimming.

Prepare the brains as on page 147, but use 3 parts water to 1 part
vinegar instead of the mixture suggested there. Cook the lamb
bones with the vegetables and seasonings slowly, for about 1½
hours. Add the drained brains and cook very gently for another 20
minutes. Strain off the stock, discarding bones and whole vegetables. Cut the brains into small pieces and return them to the stock.
Heat and serve on slices of fried bread. Add garlic purée or pepper
sauce (though the latter is not traditional) to taste.

Avgolemono Soupa

Egg & lemon soup
Greece and Cyprus

Beloved egg and lemon mixture! You will find many variants in this book. Here it is a simple, delicious soup, both light and nourishing. The stock is most often made with chicken, but it can also be made with fish or beef, and there is no reason at all why it should not be made with vegetables.

4 tablespoons long-grain rice
1.75 litres/3 pints stock
2 large or 3 small eggs
the juice of 2 lemons

2 tablespoons parsley, finely chopped
salt and freshly ground black pepper to taste

Wash the rice and cook it in the stock until tender. Remove from heat to cool a little. Now beat the eggs until frothy, adding the lemon juice and 1 tablespoon of cold water. Slowly add to this a spoonful of the stock, whisking well all the time, and then another spoonful, and then a third. Now incorporate the egg mixture in the body of the stock, whisking the while. Heat gently, stirring constantly, but in no circumstances allow to boil. (The eggs would curdle.) Just before serving, shower in the parsley and season.

Youvarlakia

Greece

This is the soup with meatballs. It also involves the *avgolemono* method (see above).

450 g/1 lb lamb, finely minced
1 small onion, finely chopped
2 eggs, beaten
50 g/2 oz long-grain rice
2 tablespoons parsley, finely chopped
salt and black pepper to taste

flour for coating
1.75 litres/3 pints stock
2 more eggs
the juice of 2 large or 3 small lemons
1 tablespoon parsley, finely chopped

Mix the lamb, onion, eggs, rice, parsley and seasoning. Shape into small balls and roll lightly in flour. Bring the stock to the boil. Put the meatballs in it. Cover and simmer very gently for about 1 hour, until cooked. Remove the meatballs and carefully keep warm. Now follow the *avgolemono* method (see opposite) of beating the eggs with lemon juice and 1 tablespoon of cold water, and incorporating in the stock. Replace the meatballs in the soup; heat it up, if necessary, and serve garnished with parsley.

Variation: You could serve the meatballs in a sauce rather than as a soup. To do this, cook the meatballs in just enough stock or water to cover them. Remove the meatballs to a serving dish and make avgolemono sauce, following the recipe on page 158, and using the strained liquid the meatballs have been cooked in.

Trahanas

Burghul & yogurt soup
Greece & Cyprus (and elsewhere)

Versions of this excellent soup exist all over the Middle East and in the Balkans, too.

It is made from burghul mixed with sour milk or yogurt and left to ferment. It is then salted, spread out to dry on a cloth – often on a flat roof – and later chopped into rough pieces and stored for winter soups. It doesn't sound immediately appetizing but, if the soup is properly made, it's delicious . . . and wonderfully nourishing and sustaining, as well as easy to digest.

I hold firm views on *trahanas*, which is available in Britain from Oriental and Greek Cypriot provision stores. The chunks are packed in plastic bags. In Britain, a powder in packets is also available, praised as making a 'smoother' soup. Cypriot friends of mine deplore this idea, and so do I. The soup should not be a cream; it should be an extremely thin porridge, with just a trace of a nutty texture. Those who like the 'smooth soup' recommend very meagre quantities of *trahanas* in their recipes. In my view, this is a mistake.

As well as being eaten by ordinary people (like me!) with enjoyment, the soup is often given to children and to invalids because of its healthiness.

1.5 litres/2½ pints chicken or
   meat stock

250 g/9 oz *trahanas* pieces
salt to taste

Rinse the *trahanas* thoroughly in a large sieve. Then place it in a heavy pan with the stock or water. Leave to stand for at least 20 minutes. Now break up the *trahanas* with a potato masher or a fork. Put on the stove with salt – I use a teaspoonful – and bring to the boil, stirring quite often. Reduce to a low heat and simmer for 30 minutes, stirring frequently to prevent any sticking.

Your basic soup is ready. It can now be served – almost invariably with lemon quarters to squeeze into it. Some people like to add a little olive oil; others add diced Haloumi cheese. Sometimes pieces of the meat (never pork) or chicken which has been used to make the stock are served with the soup.

The friend with whom we first made *trahanas* soup, Androula Costi, says that her family like a little rice in it. For this, you would add 50 g (2 oz) washed long-grain rice to the soup 12 minutes before it is cooked – you may also have to add a little more stock or water.

I prefer the *trahanas* without any of the additions listed above. I like – as many Cypriots do – to 'avgolemonize' it: a very simple matter:

1 egg
juice of 1 large or 2 small
   lemons

When the soup is cooked, take it off the heat. In a mixing bowl, using a whisk, beat the egg with the lemon juice and 1 tablespoon of cold water until foamy. Add a ladleful of the soup, then two or three more, whisking as you do it. Then incorporate this mixture – whisking constantly – into the soup.

Any leftover soup can be reheated over very low heat. Do not allow to boil, particularly if you have added egg. The addition of 150 ml/¼ pint of extra liquid will be necessary, because the soup thickens as it cools. Note: If you *don't* 'avgolemonize', I would say that it is almost essential to add lemon juice to your bowl of soup at the table.

Revythia me tahini

Chick pea soup
Cyprus

250 g/8 oz chick peas
the juice of 2 lemons
2 cloves of garlic, crushed
100 g/4 oz tahini
1¼ litres (2 pints) stock or
    water

1 tablespoon finely chopped
    parsley
salt and freshly ground black
    pepper

Prepare and cook the chick peas as follows. Soak them overnight, after washing and picking them over. After soaking, if you stir them around in a lot of cold water, the skins will float to the surface and can be skimmed off. Now drain them, and bring them to the boil in fresh water. Change the water again, and simmer until tender. This will take at least an hour, more if they are old. You can, of course, substitute tinned chick peas, with their liquid. Then purée them in the food processor with the lemon juice, garlic and tahini. Bring the stock to the boil, remove it from the heat and add a ladleful to the hummus mixture. Then incorporate the mixture in the liquid. Heat gently, taste for seasoning and serve garnished with parsley.

Variation: Some people add 1 tablespoon of tomato purée. This soup is often served with lemon wedges, and some people like to add a trickle of olive oil to it at the table.

Kakavia

Fish soup
Greece

I, and many other people, like to think of this as the original of bouillabaisse, though it is rougher than what you will be offered in Marseilles. It is a fisherman's soup, which I first encountered on the island of Aghios Nikolaos. It is an adaptable soup, its ingredients being dictated by necessity. Go to the fish market and chose firm white fish such as cod and haddock. Red mullet is good, too. I have included plenty of seasoning not always available.

3 onions, coarsely chopped
450 g/1 lb tomatoes, diced
3 cloves of garlic, crushed
chopped celery tops
2 large potatoes, peeled and
    chopped
2 bay leaves
1 tablespoon parsley, finely
    chopped
1 teaspoon *rigani* (origanum)

1 teaspoon thyme, finely
    chopped
a sprig of rosemary
the juice of two lemons
150 ml/¼ pint olive oil
1.75 litres/3 pints water
salt and pepper to taste
1 kg/2¼ lb assorted fish,
    cleaned

Put all the ingredients except the fish in a large pot. Bring to the boil and allow to simmer slowly for 1 hour. Add the fish and cook for another 30 minutes. This is often served over slices of bread.

Fassolia soupa

Haricot bean soup
Greece and Cyprus

Bean soups can be found beyond the Hellenic world but, to me, they will always be associated with it. Even today, in Limassol, passing the most modest café at about noon, you will see a couple of workmen having an early lunch. On the table between them is a whole, round crusty loaf, with two raw onions and a halved lemon, and they are eating bowls of this soup.

450 g/1 lb white (haricot)
    beans
2 or 3 carrots, sliced
2 medium onions, peeled and
    chopped
celery stalks and leaves,
    chopped (optional)
1.5 litres/2½ pints water

150 ml/¼ pint olive oil
1 teaspoon sugar
3 or 4 tomatoes, peeled and
    diced, or 2 tablespoons
    tomato paste
salt and freshly ground pepper
1 tablespoon parsley, chopped

Soak the beans and bring them to the boil, afterwards throwing away the water, as described on page 75. Now put all the ingredients into a heavy pan, except fresh tomatoes and seasonings. Cover with hot water. Cook slowly for at least 1½ hours, adding more water if necessary. About 30 minutes before serving, add the fresh tomatoes, if used, or stir in the tomato paste, diluting it with a little of the soup first, and add salt and pepper to taste.

This soup is a real meal. Some people squeeze lemon juice into it. Others add wine vinegar.

Louvana

Split pea soup
Cyprus

225 g/8 oz yellow split peas
900 ml/1½ pints water
2 onions, chopped
4 tablespoons olive oil

2 medium potatoes, cut into
   cubes
salt and freshly ground black
   pepper

After washing, soak the split peas overnight. Drain and rinse them and put them in a heavy pan with the water. Bring to the boil and skim if necessary. Cover and simmer over low heat for about 1 hour. Meanwhile, fry the onions in the olive oil until soft and golden. Add them with the raw potatoes to the peas. Cook until very tender, up to a further hour. Now season, and either pass through a mouli or process to a smooth purée.

Split pea soup is traditionally served with bread, black olives and wedges of lemon to squeeze into it. Some people add extra olive oil at the table.

TWO TOMATO SOUPS

I am very fond of fresh tomato soups, so here are two: one from the Lebanon and one from Greece.

—— *Shurbat banadoura ma' shabitt* ——

Tomato soup with dill
Lebanon

2 onions, thinly sliced vertically
2 cloves of garlic, crushed
50 g/2 oz unsalted or clarified butter
1 kg/2¼ lb tomatoes, peeled and chopped
1.75 litres/3 pints water

1 tablespoon tomato paste
½ teaspoon dill
salt and freshly ground pepper

garnish:
2 tablespoons parsley, finely chopped

In a heavy saucepan cook the onions with the garlic in the butter until soft. Add the tomatoes and simmer for 15 minutes. Now add the water and the other ingredients. Stir well, bring to the boil and simmer for a further 30 minutes. Garnish with parsley, and serve.

—— *Domato soupa* ——

Tomato soup
Greece

1 kg/2¼ lb ripe tomatoes, peeled
3 tablespoons olive oil
1 medium onion
1 clove of garlic, crushed
1 potato
1 courgette

2 tablespoons olive oil
1 litre/1¾ pints water
1 teaspoon sugar
¼ teaspoon cinnamon
salt and freshly ground black pepper
1 tablespoon parsley, chopped

Chop the vegetables and cook them in the oil till soft. Blend in the food processor. Add them to the water, with the sugar and seasonings and bring to the boil. Simmer for 10 minutes, and scatter with parsley before serving.

Shurbat ades ma' sha'riya

Lentil and vermicelli soup
Lebanon

Combinations of grain and pasta, as well as of different kinds of grain, are popular in the Middle East. This soup is a good example of the former.

225 g/8 oz brown lentils
1 litre/1¾ pints chicken stock
200 g/7 oz vermicelli, broken up
2 onions, finely sliced
2 tablespoons olive oil or unsalted butter

1 clove of garlic, crushed with 1 teaspoon coriander seeds
salt and freshly ground black pepper

Wash the lentils thoroughly. Cover them with the stock and cook until tender, adding the vermicelli for 10 minutes at the end, and adding a little more stock if necessary. Sauter the onions in the oil and add to the pot, with the garlic and coriander. Season to taste. Simmer for a minute or two and serve.

Madzounabour

Yogurt soup
Armenia

750 ml/1¼ pints yogurt, stabilized (see page 187)
900 ml/1½ pints chicken or vegetable stock or water
salt and freshly ground black pepper

15 g/½ oz butter
1 small onion, finely chopped
2 teaspoons dried mint, crushed
1 egg, beaten (optional)

Heat the stabilized yogurt on a low heat, stirring continuously, with a wooden spoon, until it just comes to the boil. Gradually add the stock, stirring constantly. Season with salt and pepper, and leave to simmer on a low heat.

Melt the butter in a small pan. Add the onion and mint and cook until the onion is soft. Pour into the soup, bring to the boil and simmer gently for a few minutes. If you wish to enrich with egg, beat the egg thoroughly, and stir into it a little of the soup. Add to the soup, but do not allow to boil.

This soup can be garnished with croûtons of bread, fried in oil, or with a scattering of chopped parsley.

─── *Cold cucumber and yogurt soup* ───

Cold soups are a comparatively new development in the Middle East, but, like everyone else, people here are responsive to fashion. The ingredients give a traditionally Middle Eastern quality.

900 ml/1½ pints yogurt
2 medium cucumbers, wiped
   but not peeled
2 cloves of garlic, crushed

½ teaspoon dried mint,
   crumbled
salt and freshly ground black
   pepper

Beat the yogurt until thin. Add the other ingredients and blend thoroughly, seasoning to taste. Cover and chill.

─ *Granny Williamson's simple summer soup* ─
Turkey

This refreshing soup does not sound Middle Eastern, but Mrs Williamson brought it from Smyrna, in Turkey.

300 ml/½ pint yogurt
300 ml/½ pint tomato juice
the juice of 1 large orange (if it
   is very sweet, add 1 teaspoon
   lemon juice)
3 or 4 fresh mint leaves

salt and freshly ground black
   pepper

garnish:
1 tablespoon parsley, finely
   chopped

Blend the yogurt and tomato juice. Add the other ingredients, seasoning to taste, and blend again. Chill well, and serve garnished with the chopped parsley.

EGGS

FOR MANY YEARS, eggs have played an important role in my cooking, giving the necessary 'airiness' of texture to soufflés and mousses. I am also fond of conjuring up a light little omelette in a few minutes.

This is not the way eggs are treated in Middle Eastern cookery. Except in my beloved avgolemono, they are not used to lighten, but to enrich, and the Arabic *eggah* (pronounced 'edger' except in Egypt), though usually defined as an omelette, is more like a cake. It can contain vegetables, pasta, chicken or even meat.

I have never cared for the combination of eggs and chicken (is this an incest taboo?), though I make an exception for chicken livers. Nor, with rare exceptions such as moussaka (page 140) do I enjoy dishes containing both meat and eggs. As a result my choice of Middle Eastern egg dishes tends to be almost entirely vegetarian.

Bayd Hamine

Hamine eggs
Egypt

Hard-boiled eggs are very popular in the Arab countries of the Middle East. (Sometimes, after hard-boiling, they are deep fried.) People dip the eggs in a mixture of salt and cumin. Try this, as an alternative to plain salt, on your next picnic.

Hamine eggs, quintessentially Egyptian, are hard-boiled eggs to the nth degree. In Egypt, they are sometimes served in the shell, as above, with salt and cumin. Traditionally, though, they are most often served shelled – their whites have become a pale brown – with *ful medammes* (see page 75). It is economical to serve them on an occasion when you need a lot: the six-hour cooking seems wasteful for just a few.

eggs
oil
onion skins

Put the eggs in a large saucepan half-filled with water. Add the skins of three or four large onions. Some people add a little ground coffee so that the shells will be even darker. Adding 1 or 2 tablespoons of oil to the water will slow down the evaporation of the water during cooking.

Bring very gently to the boil. Then cover and simmer over an extremely low heat for about 6 hours. (Check from time to time to see if you need to add more water.) Allow to cool before serving. These eggs have an exotic colour and a unique taste and texture.

Bayd Mahshi

Stuffed eggs
Egypt

This way of stuffing eggs makes a change from the usual anchovy or Marmite mixtures.

6 hard-boiled eggs	salt and freshly ground black
2 tablespoons yogurt	pepper
1 small onion, grated	12 black olives, stoned
1 pickled cucumber, grated	

Halve the eggs and remove the yolks. Mash the yolks with all the other ingredients except the olives. Fill the whites with the mixture, and top each with a black olive.

Çilbir

Eggs with yogurt
Turkey

As in the previous recipe – and the following one – yogurt here establishes a very pleasing relationship with eggs.

Many variations on this dish are possible. The eggs themselves can either be cooked until set in 40 g/1½ oz butter or poached. I like them poached. They can be served on a bed of stewed onions or on toast. I like them on a bed of spinach (a healthy alternative to *Oeufs pochés Florentine*) or on their own, with some good bread.

6 fresh eggs
300 ml/½ pint yogurt
salt and freshly ground black
  pepper
½ teaspoon cumin
2 teaspoons paprika
40 g/1½ oz melted unsalted
  butter

Poach the eggs and arrange them on a hot serving dish. Beat up the yogurt with the salt, pepper and cumin, and pour it over the eggs. Mix the paprika with the melted butter and trickle it on top. Serve at once.

Laban bil-bayd

Eggs with yogurt
Lebanon

These eggs, baked in a hot yogurt and garlic sauce make an exciting first course.

2 to 3 cloves of garlic
salt and freshly ground black
  pepper
2 teaspoons dried mint,
  powdered
50 g/2 oz unsalted butter
500 ml/18 fl oz heated and
  stabilized yogurt (see page
  187)
6 eggs

Crush the garlic with salt and the mint. Cook it for 3 minutes in the heated butter, stirring frequently.

Pour the hot yogurt into six ramekins. Then break an egg into each. Top with the garlic, mint and butter mixture. Bake until egg whites are just firm in a hot oven (220°C/425°F/gas 7).

─────────────── *Menemen* ───────────────

Eggs with vegetables
Turkey

This dish is reminscent of the Provençal *pipérade* . . . and delicious.

6 large assorted peppers (red, green, purple and yellow)
2 medium onions
50 g/2 oz unsalted butter or 3 tablespoons olive oil

450 g/1 lb tomatoes
6 eggs
salt and freshly ground pepper

Remove seeds, core and pith from the peppers and cut them into short, thin strips. Slice the onions finely, vertically. Cook together in the butter or oil until soft. Add the peeled and chopped tomatoes. Cook for a few minutes until the tomatoes have merged with the other vegetables. Cool slightly, and then add the beaten eggs, seasoned to taste. Cook over very low heat, stirring gently, until the eggs are just set. Serve at once.

Variation: Some people add 100 g/4 oz Feta cheese, crumbled into the eggs, but I don't recommend this.

─────────────── *Avga me horta* ───────────────

Eggs with fresh greens
Cyprus

I have described elsewhere (page 83) how wild greens are often gathered by the whole family on 'Clean Monday' in Cyprus. Wild asparagus, young mallow plants, dandelion leaves or spinach could be used to make this simple dish in Britain. However, I think it is best of all made with *glysterida*, the fleshy-leafed plant which grows like a weed in Cyprus during the summer. In Britain, it is called purslane. (See page 116).

purslane, spinach or other fresh
    greens – a good bunch
2 tablespoons olive oil or 40
    g/1½ oz butter
4 eggs
salt and freshly ground black
    pepper to taste

If you can get hold of purslane, use the fleshy leaves at the top of the plant. Otherwise, shred the leaves of young greens, or chop the tops of wild asparagus. Cook briskly in the oil or butter until wilted. Beat the eggs with salt and pepper, and pour them over the greens. Do not attempt to 'fold' the resulting 'omelette'. Serve it from the pan as soon as the eggs have set.

Bayd ma' akbad al-dajaj

Eggs with chicken livers
Lebanon

A 'fry-up'? I suppose so, but the addition of cinnamon and parsley make it seem different.

225 g/8 oz chicken livers,
    diced
50 g/2 oz unsalted butter
salt and freshly ground black
    pepper
a good pinch of cinnamon
6 eggs
1 tablespoon parsley, finely
    chopped

Sauter the chicken livers in the hot butter in a large pan. Break the eggs over them – carefully – and fry till set. Sprinkle with salt, pepper and cinnamon and garnish with parsley. Serve from the pan.

Variation: Fried eggs are often sprinkled with sumac (see page 186); you could replace the cinnamon with it in this recipe.

Kousa ma' bayd bil-furn

Marrow with eggs
Lebanon

It is the spices that turn this dish into something extraordinary. The eggs take on almost a mushroom colouring. And the fact that the eggs are not 'set' in the pan with the vegetables results in a lighter texture than that of most *eggahs*.

450 g/1 lb young marrow or courgettes
2 medium onions, chopped
2 cloves of garlic, crushed
50 g/2 oz unsalted butter
8 eggs
1 teaspoon allspice
½ teaspoon nutmeg
salt and freshly ground black pepper
breadcrumbs

Peel the marrow or courgettes and chop small. Sauter the onion and garlic in the butter until golden brown. Add the marrow and cook until tender. Leave the mixture to cool a little, while you beat the eggs lightly with the seasonings. Fold the eggs into the vegetable mixture and put into a buttered casserole. Sprinkle with breadcrumbs. Bake in an oven preheated to 450°F/230°C/Gas mark 8 for 15 minutes.

Some thoughts on the eggah

Provided one excises the word 'omelette' from one's mind and approaches this dish as if it were a savoury cake or a pie in which the egg takes the place of pastry, it can be an enjoyable experience.

The filling is all-important. As I said earlier, I don't like eggs with a meat or chicken filling, so vegetable *eggahs* seem to me the most satisfactory. And the filling must be moist and well-seasoned. I almost invariably include onions and/or garlic, and sometimes grated cheese.

The *eggah*, found all over the Middle East but particularly in Egypt, is excellent stuffed in pitta halves. It can be eaten cold – in which case it is better made with olive oil than with butter. It is usually served cut into wedges.

The constants are as follows:

6 eggs
50 g/2 oz unsalted butter or
  2½ tablespoons olive oil
salt and freshly ground black
  pepper

1 tablespoon parsley, finely
  chopped

Filling
You will need 450 g/1 lb filling: this could be leeks, boiled and
drained spinach, tomatoes, courgettes or aubergines. Any of these,
except the leeks, can be combined with onions. Cook the filling in
30 g/1 oz unsalted butter or about 1½ tablespoons extra-virgin
olive oil.

Beat the eggs with the seasonings and parsley. Heat the
remaining butter or oil in a heavy frying pan, combine the filling
and the egg and cook on a very low heat until firmly set.

FISH

FISH IS THE great culinary passion of my life, vouched for by the fact that I have written three books on fish cookery. These books have included recipes from the Middle East, though the region cannot be called rich and varied in its fish cookery.

Grilling predominates, closely followed by frying, and sauces are few and simple. However one has no cause for complaint when offered dishes like the ones that follow.

Samak bi-tahina

Fish with tahini
Lebanon

1 large fish (grouper would probably be used locally, but sea-bass or bream are good substitutes) weighing about 1 kg/2¼ lbs
1½ teaspoons salt

4 tablespoons olive oil
2 medium onions, finely chopped
the juice of a large lemon
4 tablespoons water
6 tablespoons tahini

Clean the fish and rub it all over with the salt. Refrigerate for several hours. When it is time to start cooking, bring out the fish and allow it to reach room temperature. Brush it with olive oil, and bake in a preheated oven (190°C/375°F/gas 5) for 20 minutes. Now carefully skin the fish. Fry the onions in olive oil till they take colour.

Beat the lemon juice and water into the tahini until it is creamy. Now add the fried onions. Cover the skinned fish with this sauce, and bake in the oven for a further 15 minutes.

Balik kebabi

Fish kebab
Turkey

'Kebab-ing' – probably the most famous form of Middle Eastern cookery (see page 129) – is excellent for firm fish, provided they are properly marinated and not overcooked. Swordfish is the fish most usually cooked in this way, but halibut or any other firm white fish will do. Kebabs are undoubtedly best cooked over charcoal, but can be cooked under an ordinary very hot grill.

1 kg/2¼ lb firm white fish, filleted

for the marinade:
4 cloves of garlic, crushed
2 anchovy fillets, pounded
300 ml/½ pint water
300 ml/½ pint white wine
3 tablespoons white wine vinegar

the juice of 1 lemon
2 bay leaves
½ tablespoon parsley, finely chopped
½ dessertspoon thyme, finely chopped

Cut the fish into 'bite-size' cubes and lay them in the marinade, with all the ingredients well mixed, for at least 2 hours before you skewer them. You can put rings of onion or sweet peppers between the cubes of fish on the skewer, but this is not customary, though fresh bay leaves* are sometimes used in this way. Grill the cubes, basting frequently with the marinade, and turning till they are brown on the outside, but not too soft inside (about 10 minutes).

Serve with lemons to squeeze and bread or, if you want a more elaborate meal, with Rice for Fish (see page 66) and Tarator sauce (see page 161).

* If using dried bay leaves soak them in warm water for 10 minutes first.

Barbunya Kağitta

Red mullet cooked in foil
Turkey

Although they have been so over-fished in the Mediterranean that most specimens I see nowadays look more like sardines, I cannot omit a recipe for what the Greeks call *barbouni*, the Turks *barbunya* and the Arabs *Sultan Ibrahim*. It is a fish well loved (perhaps too well loved) in these regions and, for me, will always be associated with them.

In addition, I am a keen devotee of foil or, as I call it, 'parcel' cookery, which preserves all the flavour and goodness of food, and avoids excessive reliance on fat. Now it is becoming popular in the Middle East where, in former times, the fish in the recipe that follows would have been cooked in parchment and served with the chopped herbs separate in a little bowl.

The red mullet, sometimes called 'the woodcock of the sea', is the only fish that does not actually need cleaning. However, you will probably want to clean – and, of course, scale – it, or you can get your fishmonger to do this. Leave on the head and tail.

4 red mullet, medium-sized	½ teaspoon freshly ground
1½ tablespoons olive oil	black pepper
2 tablespoons parsley, finely	½ teaspoon paprika
chopped	a good pinch of thyme
½ teaspoon salt	the juice of 1 lemon

Cut 4 pieces of foil twice as big as the fish. Rub the fish with olive oil and put them on the pieces of foil. On each fish place its share of the herbs and seasonings and the lemon juice. Fold up the parcels sealing the edges and cook in an oven preheated to 190°F/375°C/ gas 5 for 25 minutes.

Trout Maryland

Cyprus

The title of this recipe could hardly sound less Middle Eastern. Nonetheless, trout-farms are now a permanency in the Troodos mountains. Mr John Aristidou, the proprietor of two restaurants, the Maryland and now the very attractive Old Mill, in the charming mountain town of Kakopetria, cooks trout in an unmistakably local way. Mr Aristidou says his sauce is a secret. I believe the secret lies in the quality of the olive oil he uses.

8 medium trout (Mr Aristidou provides two per person)	olive oil
	lemon juice
salt and pepper	parsley, chopped

The trout are cleaned, scaled and seasoned, and then grilled, being basted once or twice with a sprinkling of olive oil and lemon juice. They are served in rather deep plates, surrounded by a little lake of oil and lemon sauce (see page 162) and scattered lightly with parsley.

You may like to serve your oil and lemon sauce in a bowl or sauceboat rather than with your trout 'swimming' in it, but I am struck by the happiness of the marriage between a 'northern' fish and this very un-northern sauce.

Psari Plaki

Greek fish
Greece

Even those who do not share my faith in the Byzantine origins of all the cookery of this region admit that this is a Greek dish. In fact it is the national way with fish. It has many variations and no one recipe for it will be the same as any other. It can include spinach, dill, mint, olives, *rigani* (the Greek version of oregano), bay leaves and breadcrumbs. Sometimes it is served hot, sometimes cold, and often in Greek fashion lukewarm. It can be cooked on top of a flame, as it often was in the old days when many people did not possess ovens, or just baked in the oven. You can make it with any firm white fish: sometimes several smaller ones, occasionally a whole large one, but most often, as here, with a large fish cut into steaks or slices. The constants seem to be tomatoes, onions and olive oil. Here is my version:

3 onions, chopped
2 carrots, sliced
1 stick of celery, sliced
2 cloves of garlic, crushed
6 tablespoons olive oil
1 kg/2¼ lb large white fish
(grouper, sea-bream, sea-
bass, cod) cut into steaks

6 tomatoes, skinned and
coarsely chopped
1 glass white wine *or* the juice
of 2 lemons
salt and freshly ground black
pepper

garnish:
2 tablespoons parsley, chopped

Fry together, till tender, the onions, carrots, celery and garlic in half the oil. Lay the fish steaks in a shallow baking dish, brushed with oil. Pour on the fried vegetables and cover with the tomatoes. Now pour on the wine or sprinkle with the lemon juice. Sprinkle on any remaining oil and season with salt and pepper. Bake for 30 minutes in the oven, preheated to 190°C/375°F/gas 5. Scatter the chopped parsley on top before serving.

Garithes me Feta

Prawns with Feta
Greece

Prawns have always been popular in the Hellenic world. Huge beauteous ones from the Gulf sometimes appear in Limassol restaurants, and are grilled on charcoal and accompanied by oil and lemon sauce (see page 162). But otherwise they tend to be more like shrimps and we fall back on frozen ones, which do very well for the dish that follows.

450 g/1 lb uncooked fresh
prawns, shelled, de-veined
and rinsed *or* 450 g/1 lb
frozen shelled prawns,
defrosted
1 large onion, finely chopped
75 ml/3 fl oz olive oil
8 spring onions, chopped
2 cloves of garlic, crushed
675 g/1½ lb tomatoes, peeled
and diced

150 ml/¼ pint dry white wine
3 tablespoons parsley, finely
chopped
½ teaspoon *rigani* or oregano
a generous sprinkling of freshly
ground black pepper
100 g/4 oz Feta cheese,
carefully sliced

Fry the onion in the oil until soft but not coloured. Add the spring onions and garlic and cook for a couple more minutes. Now add the tomatoes, wine, most of the parsley, the *rigani* and black pepper. I include no salt in this recipe because of the saltiness of the Feta cheese. Simmer for 30 minutes until reduced to a thick sauce. Put half this sauce in a casserole. Now put in the prawns and cover with the rest of the sauce. Lay slices of Feta cheese on top. (Some cooks crumble the Feta, but I think the effect is very messy.) Preheat the oven to 230°C/450°F/gas 8 and bake for 15 minutes, when the Feta will have melted and browned. Garnish with remaining parsley and serve.

Hamsi tavasi

Fresh anchovies with rice
Turkey

This and the following recipe both feature rice. The other day someone asked me for a Middle Eastern fish risotto: a dish in which small pieces of fish are cooked and mixed with rice. I am afraid I can find no such dish in Middle Eastern cuisinology, though I await correction. Fish is served *with* rather than *in* rice. See the recipe for rice to accompany fish on page 66. This is the nearest (quite a long way off!) that I can come:

1 kg/2¼ lb fresh anchovies
salt (say, 4 to 6 tablespoons)
3 small onions, chopped
100 g/4 oz butter
400 g/14 oz long-grain rice
900 ml/1½ pints boiling water
1½ teaspoons sugar
1 tablespoon sultanas

3 tablespoons freshly cracked
  walnuts, ground
1 teaspoon allspice
1 teaspoon cinnamon
1 teaspoon salt
1½ teaspoons cayenne pepper
1½ teaspoons freshly ground
  black pepper

Lay the cleaned and de-boned anchovies in a large wide pan. Cover them generously with salt so that each individual fish is well powdered inside and out. This preliminary salting – like a first stage on the route to preserving – gives the anchovies in this dish their special taste. Cover, and leave in a cool place for at least 1 hour.

Fry the onions gently in the butter until soft. Add the rice, and fry for a further 6 minutes, stirring frequently. Now pour the boiling water onto the rice, and add the sugar, sultanas, walnuts, and all the seasonings. Let these cook together for about 3 minutes. Reduce heat to a minimum. Cover the pan, and allow to simmer gently until the rice has absorbed all the liquid.

Butter a large casserole. Now wash the anchovies free of all the salt which has been covering them for at least 1 hour. Spread half of them on the bottom of the buttered casserole. Pour over the rice and its accompaniments, and lay the rest of the anchovies on top. Cover and cook in a moderately hot oven preheated to 190°C/375°F/gas 5 for about 20 minutes. Serve with any seasonable salad.

Sayyadieh

Fisherman's fish with rice
Lebanon

In Lebanese cookery, there are many fisherman's dishes. This is a very good one.

4 tablespoons olive oil	1 kg/2¼ lb fillets cod, coley,
3 medium onions, finely	haddock, hake or other non-
chopped	oily fish
900 ml/1½ pints water	450 g/1 lb long-grain rice
1 teaspoon salt	50 g/2 oz pine nuts
1 teaspoon ground cumin	the juice of 1 lemon

Heat 3 tablespoons of the oil in a large saucepan, and fry the onions until brown. Add the water, salt and cumin. Simmer until the onions have almost melted. Add the fish and cook gently for 10 minutes. Remove fish and keep warm. Now take from the stock in which the fish has been cooked sufficient to cook the rice in a separate pan until it is tender and the stock absorbed. Spoon the rice into a shallow dish and lay the fish pieces on top. Gently fry the pine nuts in the remaining tablespoon of oil until tender, and scatter them over the fish. Meanwhile simmer and reduce the remaining stock, adding the juice of a lemon. Pour this over the fish and rice or serve it separately in a small jug.

Efkolo kalamari

Simple squid
Greece

Here, and in the next four recipes I continue my crusade to make the cephalopods fully accepted and cooked in Britain. Please don't be frightened by them. The fishmongers from whom you can buy them will prepare them for you, if you ask him to remove the ink-sacs, beak and eyes. He will even chop your octopus, squid or cuttlefish for you, when this is necessary.

Here is a fisherman's simple way of cooking squid, not requiring the time needed for octopus cookery.

1 kg/2¼ lb squid, preferably small	150 ml/¼ pint olive oil
2 tablespoons wine vinegar	salt and freshly ground black pepper
1 bay leaf (optional)	3 lemons, quartered

Put the whole squid, with ink-sacs, beak and eyes removed, in a pan. Add just enough water to cover and the vinegar and bay leaf. Bring to the boil and simmer very gently for 45 minutes or until the fish is tender. Remove from the heat, drain and cool under a running cold tap. Cut into small strips about 2.5 cm/1 inch long.

Heat the olive oil in a frying pan and gently sauter the squid pieces until very lightly browned. Remove from the oil to a hot dish. Season to taste with salt and pepper, and serve with plenty of fresh lemon to squeeze over your helping.

── *Oktopodi yahni tis Kyrias Eftychias* ──

Kyria Eftychia's octopus Stew
Greece

675 g/1½ lb octopus
300 ml/½ pint olive oil
4 cloves of garlic, crushed
4 anchovy fillets
6 tomatoes, skinned and
  chopped
1 bottle red wine

3 carrots, sliced
1 bay leaf
a sprig of thyme
a sprig of marjoram
2 sticks of celery, chopped
8 shallots
6 black peppercorns

Get your fishmonger to remove the beak, eyes and ink-sac of the octopus, and to cut it into small pieces for you. At home, put it in a pan and cover with water. Bring briskly to the boil and simmer for 20 minutes. Drain and wash thoroughly in cold water.

Now heat the olive oil in a good heavy stewpan and, when just hot, put in the octopus. Cover and cook briskly for 10 minutes, stirring constantly. Reduce the heat and put in half the garlic, the anchovies and the tomatoes. Cook gently for 15 minutes. Now put in half the red wine, and add the carrots, the bayleaf, thyme, marjoram and celery. Cover and cook very slowly for 1 hour. At the end of that time, loosen the mixture with the rest of the red wine, and allow the whole to simmer for 3 long hours.

Now add the shallots, peeled but whole, and the remaining garlic. Cook for 1 hour. Just before serving, crush the 6 black peppercorns and stir them in. Serve with bread, thickly sliced.

Kalamari yahni

Squid stew
Cyprus

1 kg/2¼ lb small squid, with beak, eyes and ink-sac removed
3 large Spanish onions, finely chopped
½ tumbler strong red wine
½ tumbler dry white wine
3 bay leaves

3 cinnamon sticks
4 cloves
5 black peppercorns, crushed
1 large clove of garlic, crushed
1 tablespoon tomato paste
3 tablespoons virgin olive oil
salt

Put the squid, whole if they are very small and chopped if not, in a stewpan. Cover with water and add all the other ingredients except the olive oil and the salt. Bring to the boil and boil briskly for 15 minutes. Now reduce heat until the liquid is down to simmering point. Add the olive oil. Leave to simmer very slowly until tender and the liquid is much reduced. Squid should be tender after 1 hour's simmering, but it may take a bit longer depending on the size and age. Season with salt to taste.

Soupies yahni

Cuttlefish stew
Cyprus

I have heard that cuttlefish or *sepia*, my favourite – it is the best-flavoured – among the cephalopods, is the hardest to obtain in Britain. Persevere!

The ingredients for this stew are the same as those in the previous one, except that you should ask your fishmonger to preserve 2 of the ink-sacs for you.

The cooking method is the same as in the previous recipe except that, half way through simmering, you should put in the broken ink-sacs. Continue to cook. The stew will be a most intriguing colour.

Kalamari salata

Squid salad
Greece

Here is a cold squid dish ... still unusual in Britain.

675 g/1½ lb tiny squid
6 tablespoons olive oil
3 cloves of garlic, crushed
1 bay leaf
3 tablespoons red wine
3 tablespoons water
a generous pinch of salt

2 tablespoons lemon juice
freshly ground black pepper
   from a mill

garnish:
1 tablespoon parsley, finely
   chopped

This must be made with really tiny squid which, after cleaning and
removal of the ink-sacs, can be cut longitudinally into fine strips
instead of the familiar rings.

Sauter the squid very gently in the olive oil, with the garlic, for
about 8 minutes. Then add the bay leaf, red wine, water and salt.
Stew, with the pan covered, on a very low heat until the squid is
tender (about 30 minutes). Allow to cool, then arrange on a dish.
Sprinkle with lemon juice. Grind on some black pepper and scatter
with parsley. Chill before serving.

Psari marinato

Marinated fish
Cyprus

Can I persuade you to eat cold fried fish? I hope so. In Cyprus – as
on many of the Greek islands – there are various recipes for
preparing fried fish in sauces containing vinegar. Obviously the
origin of this was to keep a lavish catch of fish fresh for some time.
Not necessary for us today, but I like this recipe particularly. A more
common one, *Psari Savoro*, lacks the magic – and moisture – of the
tomato.

1 kg/2¼ lb small whole fish,
   cleaned and scaled, *or* fillets
   or steaks of larger firm fish
salt
flour
olive oil
3 cloves of garlic, crushed
1 teaspoon dried rosemary

1 bay leaf
2 tablespoons parsley, finely
   chopped
3 ripe tomatoes, peeled and
   chopped
150 ml/¼ pint wine vinegar
150 ml/¼ pint dry white wine
freshly ground black pepper

Rinse the fish and pat dry. Sprinkle with salt and leave to stand for 10 minutes. Now coat the fish with flour. Pour enough olive oil into a pan to cover the bottom 5 mm/¼ inch deep. Heat and fry the fish till golden brown on both sides. Remove them to a deep earthenware dish. Strain the olive oil and return to the pan. Stir in the garlic and 2 tablespoons flour, continuing till the flour colours. Now add all the other ingredients. Bring to the boil, stirring constantly. Reduce the heat and simmer for about 5 minutes. Leave to cool and pour over the fish. Serve chilled. This is sometimes eaten hot, but I think it is far better left to marinate in its sauce overnight and eaten cold.

Tarama Keftedes

Fish-roe rissoles
Greece

These, made very small, are delicious as a mezé, with drinks; larger, they provide bracing and unusual fishcakes.

100 g/4 oz smoked cod's roe
4 medium potatoes, boiled
1 medium onion, grated
2 cloves of garlic, crushed
½ tablespoon parsley, very
   finely chopped
a pinch of dried mint

a pinch of cinnamon
fresh ground black pepper

for coating:
flour

for frying:
olive oil

Mix all together, mashing thoroughly. Then leave to stand for at least 1 hour. Roll into little balls or small cakes, and roll these in flour. Deep fry in olive oil and serve hot, with lemon wedges.

Note: The cod's roe is very salty. You may want to desalinate it a bit by pouring iced water over it, and leaving it to stand for 30 minutes before draining off the water. Personally, I don't find this necessary.

GRAINS AND PULSES

I T IS WITH these ingredients that the Middle East often seems to me to have made its greatest contribution to modern eating. Originally considered the food of the poor – in contrast to meat, the ultra-desirable food of the rich – grains and pulses are now playing an ever-increasing role in the lives of the prosperous and health-conscious. Until recently, these foods have been absurdly neglected in Britain. We are making up for this now, and the Middle East is an ideal source of interesting recipes: centuries of skill and imagination have gone into presenting these 'humble' foods attractively.

GRAINS

Rice

I ought really to begin with burghul, so quintessentially Middle Eastern, but an age-old loyalty intervenes. For me, rice will always be First among (almost) Equals. Originally considered something of a luxury in the Middle East (hence the habit of using it in small quantities in conjunction with other grains and with pulses) it has now become a staple food, certainly in all the cities.

In all my Middle Eastern sojourns, savoury pilafs have comforted me. Only in Cyprus, oddly enough, is a pilaf not available at every modest restaurant.

One fact must be established. In the Middle East, rice is never just boiled. Some unsalted (or clarified) butter or oil must be added. If you are a victim of the current obsession with cholesterol, you can use less fat; you can use olive oil instead of butter. (However, rice seems to me a food which, except when eaten cold, has a particular affinity with butter.) It has never been widely popular in Britain and perhaps the reason for this is that it is so often served 'plain boiled', dreary and comfortless.

There are two main methods of cooking rice with water, salt and butter or oil. In Egypt, Turkey and Greece, the rice is fried until translucent in the butter or oil, and then the water and salt are added. In the Lebanon, the water, salt and butter are brought to the boil and then the rice is added. Undoubtedly, numerous Egyptians, Turks, Greeks and Lebanese will be queueing up to tell me I am wrong. But I firmly believe that the consensus is on my side. Both these methods achieve good results, and I suggest that one should be guided by the origin of the recipe.

Now we are faced by a far more taxing (one might even say 'mind-blowing') problem: the proportion of rice to water.

Everyone seems to be agreed that the best way to measure this is by *volume* not by weight. Rice provides the perfect justification for measurement by cup, or you can use a measuring jug to measure the rice and then the water. I suggest that we talk of cups. (If this makes you feel very nervous, take 1 cup to be the equivalent of 250 g/8 oz rice.)

Here, however, our troubles begin. Consulting three well-known authorities on Middle Eastern cookery, I come up with the following variations:

1 cup rice
1 cup water

1 cup rice
2 cups water

1 cup rice
$1\frac{1}{2}$ cups water.

With a sigh, I turn to the packet of my indestructible old friend, Uncle Ben, and find:

1 cup rice
2½ cups water

Let us try to make sense of this situation: I have tried, by testing the different proportions of rice to water and the conclusion I have come to is that nobody is *wrong*.

It depends on the quality of the rice, which, even nowadays, can vary from sack to sack. It depends on the speed of cooking, too. When cooking rice in the Middle Eastern way, what is important is that all the water should be absorbed. It is all very well to drain and strain plain boiled rice, but when rice is cooked with butter or oil, one does not want to pour this down the sink. And the rice will be 'mushy' if you use too much water, because you will cook it for too long in order to get all the water absorbed. My view is that nowadays, when most of us have supplies of boiling water 'to hand', it is sensible to err on the moderate side with the water – you can always add a little more towards the end of cooking if you find you need it. I would not presume to argue with the manufacturers of parboiled rice, but I would point out that their method is really designed to produce boiled rice, though they say that fat can be added 'if desired'.

We must start somewhere. We must use long grain rice. (Basmati is the favourite of many rice experts.) And let us wash it, first in a bowl with hot water, and then by putting it in a sieve and pouring cold water through it.

1 cup (225 g/8 oz) long-grain rice	40 to 60 g/1½ to 2 oz butter or olive oil
1½ cups water	1 teaspoon salt

1st method

Bring the water to the boil. Melt the butter or heat the oil in a saucepan, and add the rice, frying for about 3 minutes, until translucent. Add the boiling water and the salt. Allow to boil for 2 minutes. Now cover the pan, and let the rice simmer very gently until all the liquid has been absorbed: about 20 minutes. Turn off the heat and allow to stand at the side of the stove or in the bottom of the oven at the lowest possible heat for about 10 minutes. Fork it through before serving.

2nd method
Bring the water, salt and butter or oil to the boil. Add the rice. Allow to boil for 2 minutes. Now proceed as for the 1st method above.

Depending on the rice you use, you may find you have used too little water or too much. The former is easier to adjust, by adding a little from the kettle.

3rd method
There is a third method. Although Iran is right off my beat, I feel I must include *Chelau* because it is so delicious.

Chelau

Steamed rice
Iran

1 cup (225 g/8 oz) first-quality long-grain rice	1 tablespoon salt
	60 g/2 oz clarified butter
4 cups water	60 ml/2 fl oz water

Wash the rice very thoroughly and drain it. Bring the 4 cups water to the boil in a heavy saucepan (it should have a close-fitting lid, which you will need later). Add the rice and salt to the boiling water very slowly, so that the water doesn't go off the boil. Boil for 5 minutes, and then drain in a sieve.

Now, in a small pan, heat the butter and water until bubbling. Pour half of it into the saucepan in which the rice was boiled, swirling it round. Add half the drained rice, in a mound, making a hole in the centre with the spoon handle. Pour the remaining butter and water on top. Add the remaining rice. Cover with a doubled tea towel (what I call a drying-up cloth) and fit the saucepan lid on firmly. Fold the edges of the cloth up over the lid, so that it doesn't catch fire! Cook over a very low heat for 25 to 30 minutes, when the liquid will have been absorbed and the rice will be exquisitely light and fluffy.

Chelau ta dig

Steamed crusty rice
Iran

This is marvellous. To the tender lightness of the Chelau is added a crunchy golden-brown crust. This is a triumph of Persian cookery in which you can share. . . .

Follow the procedure for Chelau up to draining the rice and swirling half the butter and water mixture round the pan. Now mix a third of the rice with either:

1 egg yolk *or* 80 ml/2 fl oz of yogurt

Spread this over the bottom of the buttered pan. Mound the rest of the rice on top, add remaining butter and water, and cover, with a doubled tea towel just as for Chelau. However you must cook this version for 15–20 minutes longer. Then put the pan on a cold surface for a few minutes, before spooning the rice into a heated dish. Break up the crunchy *dig* from the bottom of the pan into small pieces and arrange these around the rice, bottom side up.

Serve rice cooked by any of these methods with grilled meat or fish, with stews, and with hot vegetable dishes. I allow 60 g/2 oz per person, but many Middle Eastern people like much more.

You can cook rice with stock instead of water. The Turks often make pilaf with rich chicken stock. You can add finely chopped onion, fried either with the rice or separately, herbs and/or spices, raisins and/or nuts. The following recipe, for rice to accompany fish, shows some of the possibilities.

Ruz lil-asmak

Rice for fish
Lebanon

4 tablespoons olive oil
½ teaspoon saffron
1 cup (225 g/8 oz) rice,
   washed
1½ cups boiling water

salt and freshly ground black
   pepper
2 tablespoons pine nuts
2 medium onions, thinly sliced
   vertically

Heat two tablespoons oil in a heavy pan. Add the saffron and then the rice. Stir and cook, bubbling, for 3 minutes. Now add the boiling water, salt and pepper. Allow to boil for 2 minutes, then reduce to very low heat. Cover and simmer for 20 minutes. Meanwhile, fry the pine nuts in the remaining two tablespoons oil. Set them aside when golden, and fry the onions until soft and brown in the same oil, adding another tablespoonful if you need it. When the rice is cooked, fork in two-thirds of the onions and pine nuts. Cover and keep warm for 10 minutes. Serve in a mound with the remaining onions and pine nuts on top.

Variation: I sprinkle the whole with half a tablespoon of finely chopped parsley but this is strictly untraditional.

There are many other rice dishes in other sections of this book (see Index). But I cannot resist giving you one more pilaf for reasons of sheer romanticism.

Ruz bil-loz wa bil-tamar

Rice with almonds and dates
Arab (origin unknown)

1 cup (225 g/8 oz) rice,
   cooked according to 1st
   Method, see page 63
50 g/2 oz butter
50 g/2 oz almonds, blanched
   and halved

8 dates, stoned (they should be
   fresh, but dried ones will do,
   if plump)
50 g/2 oz sultanas
1 teaspoon rose water (see page
   184) but this can be omitted

While the rice is standing, after cooking, melt the butter in a frying pan. Add the almonds, stirring until they turn golden. Now add the dates and sultanas, and cook, stirring, for a few more minutes. Remove from the stove and mix in the rose water, if used. Pile the rice on a dish and arrange the mixture on top of it.

Burghul

Cracked wheat

Burghul is the Arabic name for a form of cracked wheat which until recently was only found, in Britain, in health food shops and Middle Eastern and Indian provision stores, though I hear that it is now appearing in smarter supermarkets. It is quite different from English cracked, crushed or kibbled wheat, which I am not familiar with but which has apparently sometimes misled prospective purchasers of burghul.

The Turks call it *bulgur*, the Armenians call it *tzavar*, the Greeks call it *pligouri*. In Cyprus, it is called *pourgouri*, which is what I normally call it, but for your convenience, I shall refer to it here as burghul.

It is a pity that it is still not widely known in Britain, for it is a delicious, nutty-tasting grain which many people prefer to rice. It is available in two forms, fine and coarse. Recipes specify which to use.

Burghul can be eaten as an alternative to rice. When you make it into a pilaf, you use the coarse, large-grain burghul.

There are differences of opinion about washing it. Some

Cypriots say that good-quality burghul need not be washed at all, but most experts advise rinsing it with cold water in a sieve. Others wash it much more seriously (see *Prue's steamed burghul*, opposite).

As with rice, volume is most important, and I am going to use cups again. However, with burghul, there seems to be much less disagreement about the ratio of water to grain than there is in the case of rice. Almost everybody suggests 1½ cups liquid to 1 cup burghul. The use of stock instead of water produces particularly delicious results and I would advise it more strongly than I do with rice.

Let us look at a traditional (old-fashioned) way of making a burghul pilaf.

1 cup (225 g/8 oz) coarse
  burghul
75 to 100 g/3 to 4 oz butter
1 medium onion, chopped

1½ cups good chicken stock,
  seasoned with salt and freshly
  ground black pepper

Rinse the burghul with cold water in a sieve. Heat the butter in a heavy pan. Fry the onion until soft. Add the burghul, stirring to allow it to absorb the butter. Add hot stock and bring to the boil. Simmer on low heat until the stock is absorbed; about 10 minutes. Remove from heat. Cover with a tea towel, fit the lid on top of it and leave for up to 20 minutes.

Here is a modern low-fat method.

1 cup (225 g/8 oz) coarse
  burghul
1½ cups water or stock (you
  could use a stock cube)
salt and freshly ground black
  pepper

25 to 40 g/1 to 1½ oz butter
  (or olive oil, if you eschew
  butter)

Rinse the burghul with cold water in a sieve. Then put it in a pan with the hot water (or stock) and salt and pepper. Bring to the boil. Then simmer at very low heat for 10 to 15 minutes by which time the liquid will have been absorbed. Stir in the butter and leave covered for up to 20 minutes.

Your ideal recipe could lie somewhere between these two. As regards the cookery method, I would make two suggestions. I think the putting of a tea towel over the pan at the end is a good idea, and, as with rice, you could leave the burghul for its (essential) standing period at the bottom of your oven at the lowest possible heat.

Our friend, Prue Seymour, who, as well as being a wonderful cook, is dedicated to low-fat methods, suggests the following way of cooking burghul:

Prue's steamed burghul

1 cup (225 g/8 oz) coarse
    burghul
1 tablespoon olive oil
1 large onion, chopped
    medium fine

2 teaspoons powdered cumin
2 teaspoons powdered
    coriander

Wash the burghul 3 times in three lots of clean water. Then cover it with water and leave it to soak for 30 minutes.

In the oil, cook the onion with the cumin and coriander until the onion starts to brown. Remove from fire.

Sieve the soaked burghul, pressing out excess moisture. Now, in a bowl, mix it with the onions and spices, and then transfer it to a Chinese vegetable steamer (also known as a 'weight-watcher's steamer') over hot water. Cover with a cloth (and a lid, if you have one that fits) and steam for half an hour. It will do no harm to steam the burghul for even longer.

For vegetable-lovers and those interested in low-fat regimes, Prue Seymour also suggests combinations of steamed vegetables, herbs and spices to serve incorporated with the steamed burghul mixture. These are not traditional, but are Middle Eastern in terms of ingredients and style.

Cooking time must depend on the age and size of the vegetables used. Season with salt and freshly ground black pepper to taste.

i) Steam 225 g/8 oz chard (*lahana, blette*), cleaned and chopped, including the stalks, with 100 g/4 oz mushrooms which have been finely sliced, 2 cloves of garlic, finely chopped and fried in 2 teaspoons of olive oil, 1 to 2 teaspoons ground coriander, and 2 medium tomatoes peeled, de-seeded and chopped. Add to the steamed burghul mixture, and serve sprinkled with chopped fresh coriander.

ii) Steam 225 g/8 oz of shelled young peas and broad beans with 2 young carrots, finely chopped. Add to the burghul mixture and sprinkle with 1½ tablespoons parsley and 2 teaspoons of fresh mint, both finely chopped.

iii) Steam 225 g/8 oz of diced unpeeled cucumber with 225 g/8 oz of chopped spinach, 1 large red sweet pepper, de-seeded and chopped, and 1½ teaspoons powdered cardomom. Stir into the burghul mixture, and garnish with a generous sprinkling of the leaves of fresh dill, finely chopped.

Two garnishes for these delicious burghul pilafs are suggested by Prue Seymour:

Pine nuts quickly fried in a little olive oil *or*

Sesame seeds toasted by being quickly stirred in a non-stick pan over low heat.

Now, here is a Cypriot way with burghul which, like many recipes from other parts of the Middle East, includes vermicelli.

Pourgouri pilafi

Burghul pilaf
Cyprus

1 medium onion, finely chopped	1½ cups chicken stock, or water
50 g/2 oz broken-up vermicelli	salt
4 tablespoons olive oil	1 cup (225 g/8 oz) coarse burghul

In a deep pan fry the onion and vermicelli in the oil until golden. Add the chicken stock or water and bring to the boil. Wash the burghul quickly in a sieve under cold running water. Add it to the boiling liquid, with salt to taste. Stir until the mixture boils again. Then simmer, covered, over very low heat till the liquid is absorbed – about 15 minutes. Remove from heat. Cover with a cloth, and replace the lid. Allow to stand for 20 minutes.

Such pilafs, as mentioned earlier, can be served as an alternative to rice, just as burghul can be used in such a dish as *Mujaddarah* (page 80).

For a simple meal, the pilafs described above are often served accompanied by a bowl of yogurt.

The other day, I cooked a cup (225 g/8 oz) of rinsed burghul in 1½ cups of good, well-seasoned chicken stock, bringing it to the boil and simmering slowly for 15 minutes. Then I mixed in 50 g/ 2 oz butter, 1 teaspoon of cumin, half a teaspoon of red pepper, and a small onion, grated. I let this stand at the bottom of the oven, covered with a cloth and lid, for 20 minutes. Then I ate it, with a small carton of our wonderful local sheep's yogurt. A perfect lunch. . . .

A shadow falls across my page. From the delightful simplicity of a burghul pilaf, I feel forced to pass on to burghul's use in – the *kibbeh*.

Kibbeh Nayeh

Lebanon (and elsewhere)

It seems impossible to describe *kibbeh* in three or four words. They are hollow balls, torpedoes, small cylinders, with a crisp outer shell and a filling. They are made of burghul and (usually) minced meat. They frighten me.

This is partly to do with the dreariness of their traditional preparation: the endless pounding and kneading to a paste of minced lamb, burghul and onion. A *kibbeh* mixture can even be eaten raw – *Kibbeh Naye*. This is rolled into thin fingers or scooped up with lettuce leaves. I don't propose to discuss it. I have never been a fan of *steak tartare*, but at least the raw meat for that isn't endlessly handled.

Kibbeh to be cooked are reduced to the same paste-like mixture. You will now point out that a food processor can do the work. This is true. But then the paste must be rolled by hand into oval shapes, which are then hollowed, with the right forefinger until the shell is very thin, though it must not break. I hear that a machine for doing this exists, but experts say it is unsatisfactory. Apparently female skill in *kibbeh*-making (including the possession of an especially long forefinger) is valued above intellect or beauty, but it does not make *my* heart beat any faster.

This book is about 'my' Middle Eastern food, and I think this allows me to go on strike . . . once. I won't make this kind of *kibbeh* (my wife won't either) or *koupés*, the Cyprus *kibbeh* which have shells made only of burghul with a meat and onion filling.

There is however an escape and, what's more, it is a traditional one. Both *kibbeh* and *koupés* can be made 'in a tray'. This means that a layer of the outer shell material (in the former case meat and burghul, in the latter burghul alone) can be spread in a baking dish, covered with the filling, topped with another layer of the shell mixture, and baked in the oven.

I propose to offer you three tray recipes. The first has a meat-and-burghul shell and a meat filling, the second has a burghul shell and a meat filling. The third is a non-traditional variation on the second: not only the shell but also the filling is vegetarian.

Kibbeh bil-saniyeh

Kibbeh in a tray
Lebanon

1. *Meat* kibbeh *with a meat filling*

kibbeh *ingredients:*	
450 g/1 lb lean minced lamb	1 large onion
225 g/8 oz fine burghul	1 teaspoon salt
	1 teaspoon allspice

This is a recipe for which you need a processor unless you are prepared to pound the meat in a mortar until it becomes a paste. (A food processor is not essential for the two recipes that follow.)

Put the minced lamb with the onion, salt and allspice in the food processor. Using the metal blade, grind to a smooth paste.

Rinse the burghul in a sieve and then squeeze out the excess moisture. Mix the burghul with the meat and put through the food processor again.

filling:	
1 onion, chopped	stock or water
5½ tablespoons clarified or	½ teaspoon allspice
unsalted butter	½ teaspoon cinnamon
225 g/8 oz lean minced lamb	salt and freshly ground black
2 tablespoons pine nuts	pepper

The lamb for the filling does not have to be as finely ground as that used above. Indeed, there should be a contrasting texture. Fry the onion in 2 tablespoons butter until soft. Add the meat and pine nuts and cook till the meat has changed colour. Then add a little stock or water and the spices and seasonings and cook, stirring, for a few minutes more.

Now butter your cooking vessel. (The traditional baking-tray is round, but in Cyprus a square pyrex seems to be the national baking dish.) Spread half the *kibbeh* mixture over the bottom, smoothing it as you go. Top this with the filling, spread evenly. Cover with the rest of the *kibbeh* mixture, again smoothing carefully, and pressing down well. Make a diamond pattern on the top with a knife. Now dribble 3 tablespoons of melted butter over the top. Bake in an oven preheated to 180°C/350°F/gas 4 for about 50 minutes. The top should be brown and crisp.

This can be eaten hot or cold. It is traditionally served with yogurt and salads.

2. *Plain burghul* kibbeh *with a meat filling*

kibbeh *ingredients:*	300 ml/11 fl oz boiling water
450 g/1 lb fine burghul	1½ teaspoons salt

Rinse the burghul in a sieve. Put in a bowl, and pour the boiling water over it. Stir in the salt. Leave to stand for 2 to 3 hours. Now knead the mixture to a smooth paste or put it in the food processor.

You can proceed as in the first recipe, using the same filling. Or you can use olive oil instead of butter for all the cooking processes and use a Cypriot filling:

225 g/8 oz minced beef or lamb	50 g/2 oz pine nuts (optional)
1 large onion, finely chopped	a good pinch of cinnamon
1 clove of garlic, crushed	salt and freshly ground black pepper
4 tablespoons parsley, chopped	

3. *Plain burghul* kibbeh *with a vegetarian filling* (not traditional)

Make the *kibbeh* mixture as for 2 above. You can use either butter or olive oil for the cooking.
  Use the following filling:

1 large onion, finely chopped
350 g/12 oz mushrooms,
  chopped
50 g/2 oz pine nuts
50 g/2 oz almonds, blanched
  and chopped

1 tablespoon parsley, chopped
1 large ripe tomato, peeled and
  chopped (optional)

Fry all the ingredients, using either butter or olive oil. If you would like the filling to be a little more moist, add a tomato. Mix all well together, before spreading on the bottom layer of *kibbeh* mixture.
  For other burghul recipes, see index.

PULSES

White haricot beans

These are a lifelong Hellenic experience for me – served in either of the following ways.

——————— *Fassolada* ———————

Boiled haricot beans
Greece and Cyprus

Soak 450 g/1 lb white haricot beans overnight, and discard the water. Bring them to the boil in clean water – and throw that water away too. Now cover the beans with hot water. Bring to the boil and then simmer until cooked, when hardly any liquid will be left. Season with salt.
  Serve with salt, freshly ground black pepper, chopped raw onion, chopped parsley, a little olive oil and lemon wedges.

Fassolada yahni

Bean stew
Greece and Cyprus

This recipe is slightly more elaborate and even more delicious. Beans in Tomato Sauce, but how different from the image conveyed by those words in Britain.

450 g/1 lb white haricot beans
3 potatoes
2 carrots
1 medium onion
3 sticks celery (optional)

3 ripe tomatoes, peeled and
    chopped
150 ml/¼ pint olive oil
salt and freshly ground black
    pepper

Soak the beans overnight and throw away the water. Bring the beans to the boil in clean water and throw that away too. Cover the beans with hot water, bring back to the boil and let them simmer till half cooked. Now dice the potatoes, carrots, onion and celery. Add them to the beans with the tomatoes, olive oil and seasoning. Allow to simmer until everything is cooked, and there is enough thick sauce to scoop up with your bread.

To make this dish even more substantial, our friend, Mrs Rebecca Savvides, adds a few chopped rashers of streaky bacon with the rind removed.

For other haricot bean recipes, see *Fassolia Soupa* (page 36) and *Piyaz* (page 113).

Ful medammes

Fava beans
Egypt

These little brown fava beans (not in any way connected with *Fava*, page 21) are the delight which causes so many Middle Eastern writers to wax Proustian. Having no childhood memories of them, I cannot do so. They take a really unconscionable time acooking, but they *can* be bought in tins. Perhaps you should test their appeal in this form first. If you do, rinse the tinned beans and reheat in fresh water.

> 450 g/1 lb fava beans

Soak the beans overnight. Drain. Cover with unsalted water. Then simmer on top of the stove or in a very low oven (120°C/250°F/ gas ½) for from 4 to 7 hours. (You could use a slow cooker if you have one.) The length of time depends on the quality and age of the beans.

You can add crushed garlic to the beans before serving. But probably the best way is to serve them with all sorts of little garnishes from which people can help themselves:

garlic, crushed with a little salt and olive oil	salt
olive oil	freshly ground black pepper
lemon wedges	powdered cumin

The beans are often served with a finely chopped hard-boiled egg on top or, ideally – in traditional terms – with *Hamine eggs* (see page 41). Break the egg up with the beans, when eating. Alternately *ful medammes* can be served with a tomato sauce (see page 159). Or you can make a salad of them using a dressing of equal parts of oil and lemon juice, a teaspoon of cumin and salt and freshly ground black pepper. Garnish with chopped parsley and chopped spring onions. Pour the dressing over the beans while they are still warm.

Black-eyed beans

These attractive little beans need less soaking than most other beans, but you *can* soak them overnight. The following recipe shows an alternative process.

Louvia mavromatika me lahana

Black-eyed bean stew
Cyprus

225 g /8 oz black-eyed beans
750 ml/1½ pints water
450 g/1 lb *lahana* (*blette*,
  chard, silverbeet) or spinach
salt

100 ml/4 fl oz olive oil
the juice of a small lemon
2 cloves of garlic, crushed with
  a little salt (optional)

Wash the beans and cover with the water. Bring to boil and cook for 2 minutes. Remove from heat and leave for up to 2 hours. Then return to heat and simmer till tender. This will take 1 hour. Wash the *lahana* or spinach. If you use *lahana*, trim the thick stems and cut them into pieces. Add them to the beans with salt to taste and cook for a few minutes. Now add the shredded leaves or, if you are using spinach, the chopped stalks and shredded leaves. Cook for a further 15 minutes. Drain off the liquid. Put the mixture in a serving dish. Mix in the olive oil and lemon juice, with the garlic if you are using it, and serve. (I grind on plenty of black pepper.)

Louvia mavromatika me domates

Black-eyed beans in tomato sauce
Cyprus

225 g/8 oz black-eyed beans
100 ml/4 fl oz olive oil
2 medium onions, thinly sliced
  vertically
2 cloves of garlic, crushed with
  a little salt
300 ml/½ pint stock
3 ripe tomatoes, peeled and
  finely chopped

1½ teaspoons cinnamon
a good pinch of allspice
salt and freshly ground black
  pepper
1 tablespoon parsley, finely
  chopped

Soak the beans overnight, or prepare in hot water as in the previous recipe. Simmer until almost tender and drain. Heat the oil in a heavy saucepan. Cook the onions with the garlic until soft. Add the beans, stock, tomatoes and spices and simmer together for about 20 minutes. Garnish with parsley and serve. Some people squeeze lemon juice onto this at table, but I feel no need to.

Kidney beans

These decorative red beans are not used much in the Middle East, though I have come across them in a Lebanese salad (see page 114) and in the following casserole dish which can be cooked in a low oven or a slow cooker.

—————— Kidney bean casserole ——————

Given to me by a Cypriot friend, but not traditional.

225 g/8 oz red kidney beans
600 ml/1 pint water
3 tablespoons olive oil
2 medium onions, chopped
2 cloves of garlic, crushed
2 sticks of celery, chopped

1 litre/1¾ pints stock
1 teaspoon cinnamon
2 teaspoons paprika
2 tablespoons parsley, chopped
2 tablespoons currants
2 tablespoons pine nuts

Put the beans into a saucepan with the water. Cover and bring gently to the boil, then simmer for a minute or two. Allow them to stand for 2 to 3 hours. Then drain them.

Heat the oil and cook the onions, garlic and celery till soft. Put them with the beans into the casserole, with 900 ml/1½ pints of the stock. Mix in the cinnamon, paprika, parsley and currants. Cook in a low oven (160°C/325°F/gas 3) or a slow cooker, covered, for up to 3 hours. Check after 2 hours to see if it is necessary to add a little more stock. Just before serving, fry the pine nuts in a little oil till golden and sprinkle over the top.

Broad beans

These beans, so delicious fresh, never seem to me very inspiring dried. They are very popular in Egypt, where they are made into the dip, *Ful nabed*, which is their actual name in Arabic. (See page 22.) In my recipe, I advise using the skinned variety, for soaking and preparation are tedious if you buy them unskinned. I give the same advice if you are going to use them as an alternative to chick peas in *Falafel* (see below) as is often done in the Lebanon. In Cyprus, they are boiled with *lahana* (chard) and dressed with oil and vinegar, but I far prefer black-eyed beans in the very similar recipe on page 77.

Chick peas

These are very popular in the Middle East. They are of course the basis of *Hummus bi-tahina* (see page 19) and crop up in other recipes in this book. They are also usually preferred to broad beans as the basis of *Falafel*, a delicious and famous mezé (see page 24).

Yellow split peas

These need long soaking and cooking, like chick peas, but their flavour is far less interesting and they do not appear in very many recipes. The only one I can offer you is *Louvana* (see page 37).

Lentils

I am extremely fond of lentils. Because I like them *very* tender, I sometimes soak the brown ones before cooking them, but everyone else says this is quite unnecessary. Even I don't soak the red ones.

Lentils Lassalle

This is half way between a soup and a stew and I first evolved it on the island of Aghios Nikolaos and have eaten it ever since – in England and now in Cyprus. All its ingredients are Eastern Mediterranean which I feel justifies its presence here.

225 g/8 oz brown lentils
2 medium onions, chopped
3 cloves of garlic, chopped
3 tablespoons olive oil
300 ml/½ pint red wine
300 ml/½ pint water
2 tablespoons tomato paste

2 tablespoons parsley, chopped
bayleaf
stick of celery or 1 tablespoon
  celery tops, chopped
  (optional)
salt and freshly ground black
  pepper

Wash the lentils thoroughly, rinsing two or three times. You can soak them for a bit if you like. If so, drain and rinse again. Cook the onions and garlic in the olive oil till soft and golden. Now put all the ingredients in a saucepan. Bring to the boil and simmer until the liquid is almost absorbed (about 1 hour). Season to taste with salt and pepper. You may want to add a little more olive oil at the table (and I sometimes add wine vinegar, though my wife doesn't). Serve with good bread.

Mujaddarah

Lentils with rice or burghul
Lebanon

I say Lebanon, but this dish is eaten all over the Middle East, including Cyprus where it is known as *Mouchentra* or *Moujendra*. (In India, it is called *kitcheri*: the original of our very different modern kedgeree.) This is an ancient recipe; the dish is always said to be the 'mess of pottage' for which Esau sold his birthright. I can see why: though simple, it is rich, and its fragrance is extraordinarily tempting to the appetite.

As with almost all Middle Eastern dishes, proportions vary but here the basic ingredients remain constant: lentils, olive oil and salt. It is most often made with rice but coarse burghul can be substituted, giving a nuttier result. Some add black pepper: I do. Other possible additions are ground cumin, coriander, or dried mint in the cooking water. Please use a good olive oil. The dish should cool slightly before you eat it, bringing out the flavour of the oil. A thin over-refined oil will not give the dish its full quality.

Some people use equal quantities of lentils and rice or burghul. Others use a much larger quantity of lentils.

225 g/8 oz brown lentils
1 litre/1¾ pints water
1 level teaspoon cumin
2 large onions
175 ml/6 fl oz olive oil

175 g/6 oz long grain rice (or
    175 g/6 oz coarse burghul)
salt and freshly ground black
    pepper

Put the washed lentils in a saucepan with the water and cumin.
Bring to the boil and cook for about 30 minutes until almost soft.
Cut the peeled onions vertically, into half moons (or 'wings' as one
Lebanese cook poetically expresses it), thinly. Now cook half the
onions in the olive oil until soft and golden brown. Don't let them
burn. Add the washed rice or burghul and the salt, cumin and
pepper to the the lentils with the onions and most of the olive oil in
the pan. Mix in, and then simmer slowly for another 15 minutes.
Meanwhile cook the rest of the onions very slowly in the remaining
olive oil till they are almost caramelized, but not blackened. Cover
the lentil mixture and leave to stand for 10 minutes. Serve with the
onions spread on top.

Note: Some people cook the rice or burghul separately, but I haven't
found this necessary.

VEGETABLES AND SALADS

HERE, FOR MANY cooks – and eaters – in the West today – lies Middle Eastern cookery's greatest appeal. In the Middle-East vegetarian fare has been regarded by most people as penitential: necessitated either by poverty or by religious injunctions to abstain from carnivorous delights during fasts. On the other hand, among sophisticates in the West, the movement towards vegetarianism grows steadily. (Good luck to them, I say . . . only preserve me from guests who are *vegans*, though, when I come to think of it, I could offer them quite a lot of the recipes in this book.) In the field of vegetable cooking in the Middle East, however, a sense of deprivation has been a spur: cooks have exerted all their ingenuity and imagination. The results are lyrical associations of foods and flavours, and the very attractive vegetables that flourish in these regions provide perfect materials for exciting dishes.

Two Clean Mondays and a green Sunday

Don't let me convey the impression, though, that Middle Eastern people are in any way hostile to vegetables. England is (almost) always so green that one tends to take its verdancy for granted. In the Middle East, one appreciates the greenness that follows the winter rains with a particular intensity, and the fresh green foods, wild as well as cultivated, that abound in the spring are eaten with a particularly keen relish.

In Cyprus, 'Clean Monday' is the name given to the first Monday of Lent. Carnival ends on Sunday, and Monday is a holiday on which people do what is known as 'cutting the nose of Lent'. After rising early and thoroughly cleaning their houses (though it seems to me that fanatically house-proud Cypriot women do this *daily*), they collect together materials for a picnic to be eaten in the fields, where they will gather fresh wild greens as well. This is *weather permitting*: I stress the point, for most Clean Mondays I have experienced during twelve years in Cyprus have been very wet!

On Clean Monday, vegetarian fare is the rule (as, for many devout Cypriots, being Greek Orthodox, it is throughout Lent). Although fish can be added to the menu, the more serious do not do this. However, on this day it is the custom to wash down the Lenten fare with unusually lavish draughts of alcohol.

As a result of the unpredictable weather, many families – this is very much a family day – eat their midday meal in a friendly restaurant. I look back to our first Clean Monday in Cyprus – only a week or two after we had moved into our house, and before our furniture had arrived from England. Friends of ours – Michael and Penelope – were visiting Limassol, and we four strolled to the restaurant in the Public Gardens run by Mr Psara (literally, and often appropriately, 'Mr Fisherman'. We were unaware that this restaurant is always closed to the public on Monday.

As soon as we came inside we saw that the normal arrangement of tables had been altered. They had been lined up to form a giant three-sided festive board, covered with snowy tablecloths and decked with different kinds of greenery. Bottles of wine were arranged down the centre of the table and at every second place was a bottle of Cyprus whisky. A happy throng was seated and loud recorded *bouzouki* music played.

Shyly we shrank back from what was obviously a private party. But our retreat was instantly prevented. We were surrounded by Mr Psara and his friends, offering us the lavish hospitality which is so marked a feature of this country. '*Kopiaste*' ('Come and taste') is the national greeting, and, protesting feebly, we obeyed.

On the table, apart from the abundance of wild greens, were bowls of olives, a profusion of lemons, round crusty yellow loaves and many mezé dishes and there were numerous salads. After the meal, and liberal draughts of wine (we four eschewed the Cyprus whisky), there was dancing – mostly by the men. Older Cypriot women are very circumspect in this regard. However, my wife and Penelope participated to the full. In those days my Greek was rustier than it is now, and the other three did not speak Greek at all, but it would have been impossible not to feel at ease at this friendly feast. As the rain poured down outside, the red wine and the 's'agapo' music were equally warming. (In Greek popular music, the words 's'agapo' crop up quite as often as do their English counterparts – 'I love you' – in British songs.) It was early evening before we returned by taxi to our house. There had, inevitably, been no bill. We had been invited to a party in Nicosia, but we decided that we would have a short rest before setting forth. However, none of us – Michael and Penelope shared an ancient mattress waiting to be collected by the dustmen – woke until the small hours.

The second Clean Monday which sticks in my memory is a quieter one. We had made up a small party to go to the Archipelago, a restaurant which, as far as I know, never closes. It nestles between the hillside on which stood the ancient city of Amathus (site of some of the country's most thrilling archaeological discoveries) and the small chapel of Aghia Varvara. On that Clean Monday, several years ago, there were no buildings beyond Aghia Varvara. Now, monstrous Sheratons and Meridiens stretch into the distance, and one wonders how long the Archipelago, the ancient city, even the old chapel can survive the encroaching 'developers' whose bulldozers, like savage rottweilers, worry the edges of the marvellous site, between sea and . . . motorway.

The Archipelago is in a small, unpretentious building. In summer, one eats outside, under the swelling bunches of grapes on a great vine; in winter, inside by an open fire on which grilling of impeccably fresh fish takes place. The proprietor has a bohemian air. Bearded and bereted, he could be a French intellectual. Instead, he is a splendid cook of fish and of *kleftiko* (page 127) in an outdoor sealed oven.

Many families sat at tables, almost concealed by the mounds of greenery they had brought with them. It had – of course – been raining, but after lunch a pale sun emerged, shedding watery light on the sea and the slope of the ancient city. There was no dancing, but two guitars were played, and there was gentle singing in the fading sunlight and the dim glow of one or two oil lanterns. (In those days, the Archipelago had no electricity.) A delicious melancholy pervaded me. Lines of Cavafy drifted through my mind as I nibbled on a sprig of charlock. . . .

I treasure a third (largely vegetable) occasion: one of the hallowed Easter Sunday picnics held by Prue and Ian Seymour at their country retreat, which is perched on a steep slope above the village of Vizakia. (At night, the delicate but insistent tinkle of goat bells is borne upward.) The little house, initially surrounded by bare earth and stones but now by Prue's ever more bosky garden, faces the astonishingly variegated foothills of the Troodos range. To the right is a glimpse of the sea at Morphou (currently inaccessible, alas, as a result of the Turkish invasion). One is also conscious that, a few miles to the left, at the end of a valley of pines, is the thrilling church of Panaghia tou Asinou. Outside, it is a stone box with a pitched roof; the door opens on a jewel case: walls and ceiling are entirely covered with glowing frescoes dating from the 11th century.

To Prue's picnics, her friends, who are from all over the Middle East – and especially from the Lebanon – bring wondrous dishes: a giant *tabbouleh* (see page 111), a magnificent *fattoush* (see page 110) and the Assyrian triumph *bazergan* (see page 112). Such dishes are happily partnered by glasses filled, by ladle, from a small bath (Prue puritanically insists that this is a 'large bowl') of Ian's inimitable Bloody Marys. But I digress. . . .

Cooked vegetable dishes are not always instantly distinguishable from salads in the Middle East, as many of them can be – and are – served cold. They often form part of the mezé course; raw salads almost invariably do, never accompanying or following hot main dishes but always preceding them. Of course, if such an eating pattern doesn't suit you, you can adopt a more compatible one. I will make a working division here between cooked vegetables and salads.

Stuffed vegetables

These are perhaps the best known form of Middle Eastern vegetable cookery. The mystique – especially among the Arabs and Turks – is tremendous, and endless subtle variations are presented.

The Turks call stuffed vegetables *dolma*; to the Arabs, they are *mahshi*. The Greeks use the word *dolmades* for stuffed vine leaves and cabbage leaves but, like the Cypriots, use the word *yemista* for stuffed vegetables. The Cypriots do not speak of *dolmades*; they call stuffed vine leaves *koupepia*, which means 'little cigars'!

Stuffed vegetables can be eaten hot or cold. If they are to be eaten cold, meatless fillings are usually preferred, and olive oil is used instead of butter.

The first time I cooked stuffed vegetables I was terrified. When cooked, they were delicious – so guests said – but they had a rather battered appearance. I had cooked them on top of the stove in a deep saucepan, and they went out of control, lurching drunkenly around. Since then I have learnt to put a plate on top of them (as described in some of the recipes that follow) but usually nowadays I cook them in the oven in a baking dish where, lying down, they are submissive.

Preparing the vegetables is half the battle ... the duller half.

Aubergines
Wash them. Cut off a small piece at each end and discard. Cut the aubergines in half (this is simpler) or cut them down one side, if you want the effect of a whole aubergine. With an apple corer, scoop out the flesh, but leave a lining 6 mm/¼ inch thick inside the skin. Otherwise, the aubergines will fall apart. In Cyprus, we throw away the extracted flesh. You could use it in a soup or stock. What you mustn't do, when filling with rice or burghul mixtures, is to incorporate it in the filling. There are other recipes where the flesh is used. (See *Imam bayildi*, page 95). But, with grain, the result would be messy.

Now immerse the aubergines in cold salted water, to which you have added the juice of a lemon, for at least 10 minutes. Dry them with a cloth. *Optional:* you can sauter the aubergines lightly in a little olive oil, before stuffing them.

Courgettes
Wash them. Cut off the stalk end. If large, cut them in half. If small, stuff them whole. Remove the flesh carefully with an apple corer, as for aubergines, again leaving a lining. Discard the inner flesh or use in soup or stock. *Optional:* you can now sauter the courgettes very briefly in olive oil.

Onions
Peel them carefully. Put in a pan and cover with water. Bring to boil.

Cook until softened, but not breaking up. You should now be able easily to remove and discard the centre of the onion, except one layer which press inside the outer layer to form a cup.

Sweet peppers
Put in a pan and pour boiling water over. Remove end, and inner seeds and pith. *Optional:* you can very briefly and carefully sauter the pepper in olive oil.

Tomatoes
Slice off a cap, or leave it attached at one side. Remove inside with a teaspoon, leaving a lining. If you are one of the no-seeds brigade, you can sieve the pulp and flesh. *Keep* them, in any case.

Now fill the vegetables. Put on the tomato caps. Use one of the two fillings given below, leaving a little room at the top for expansion. Put in an oiled baking dish and pour seasoned stock (to which you could add a little tomato juice and a small piece of cinnamon bark) a third of the way up the vegetables. Cover with foil and bake for half an hour at 190°C/375°F/gas 5. Remove the foil and baste with the liquid. Cook for another 15 to 20 minutes.

Fillings
The quantities given should be enough for 18 medium-sized vegetables.

Filling I – with meat

1 large onion, finely chopped
3 tablespoons olive oil
1 kg/2¼ lb beef or lamb, finely minced
100 g/4 oz short-grain rice
flesh and pulp of tomatoes for stuffing plus, if necessary, a couple more tomatoes (the final mixture should be moist but not runny)

2 tablespoons parsley, chopped
1 teaspoon dried mint
salt and freshly ground black pepper

Soften the onion in the heated oil. Add the mince, and cook until it changes colour. Add the washed rice and cook for a few minutes more, before adding the tomato pulp, herbs and seasoning. Mix well.

A vegetarian suggestion: substitute 675 g/1½ lb minced mushrooms for the minced meat.

———— *Filling II – without meat* ————

170 g/6 oz short-grain rice, washed and drained
3 tomatoes, peeled and finely diced
1 large onion, finely chopped
3 tablespoons parsley, finely chopped
3 tablespoons pine nuts
1½ tablespoons raisins
1½ teaspoons salt
½ teaspoon freshly ground black pepper
½ teaspoon powdered cinnamon

Put all the ingredients together and knead thoroughly.

I can't stress too strongly how many variations you can devise, using nuts, raisins and all the spices of Arabia. Rice can be replaced by coarse burghul or by cooked chick peas mashed up with various savoury ingredients.

Here is an Egyptian recipe for stuffed cabbage with a sauce.

———— *Korumb mahshi* ————

Stuffed cabbage leaves
Egypt

leaves from 2 medium cabbages
1 medium onion, finely chopped
2 cloves of garlic, crushed
25 g/1 oz butter
450 g/1 lb finely minced beef
175 g/6 oz short-grain rice
2 teaspoons dill, finely chopped
½ teaspoon ground cumin
2 tablespoons tomato paste
salt and freshly ground black pepper

for the sauce:
4 tablespoons tomato purée
100 ml/4 fl oz meat stock
the juice of ½ lemon
½ teaspoon sugar
salt and freshly ground black pepper
50 g/2 oz butter

Use medium-size cabbage leaves. Blanch them in boiling salted water till they are just pliable enough to roll. Drain. Remove the central stems and use these to line a heavy saucepan, together with any damaged or tough outer leaves. (This prevents your cabbage rolls sticking.)

Fry the onion with the crushed garlic in butter until soft. Mix with uncooked mince and rice and the other filling ingredients.

Stuff the halved cabbage leaves, placing about 1 tablespoonful on each, and making a neat package with the sides tucked in. Arrange these on the stems, in the pan. Combine all sauce ingredients (except the butter) and pour them over the cabbage rolls. Dot with the butter. Place a heavy plate upside down on top of the rolls. Cover the pan and simmer at a low heat for 1 hour. Serve hot.

Mahshi malfouf bil-zayt

Meatless stuffed cabbage
Lebanon

There are many Middle Eastern variations on the theme of stuffed cabbage leaves. But a vegetarian one is hard to find. In this Lebanese version, rice and chick peas, combined, replace the meat.

I have suggested using tinned chick peas because, with the small quantity required (225 g/8 oz *cooked* weight), it hardly seems worthwhile going through the chick pea cooking process, but you can, of course, do so. (If you make some hummus (page 19) at the same time, you could cook extra chick peas.)

1 good-sized cabbage (not a huge one)
2 medium onions, *or* 2 bunches spring onions, finely chopped
50 ml/2 fl oz olive oil
170 g/6 oz long-grain rice, washed and drained
225 g/8 oz tinned (or cooked) chick peas, drained
2 tablespoons parsley, finely chopped

3 medium tomatoes, peeled and chopped finely
1/2 teaspoon allspice
salt
freshly ground black pepper

for the sauce:
3 or 4 cloves of garlic, crushed
the juice of a lemon
1/2 teaspoon salt
1/2 teaspoon dried mint
50 ml/2 fl oz olive oil

Prepare and blanch the cabbage leaves as for the previous recipe, lining the pan with the cabbage stems and any coarse or damaged leaves.

Fry the onion in the olive oil, and mix with all the other filling ingredients. Use to stuff cabbage leaves.

For the sauce, mix the garlic with the lemon juice, the salt and mint. Put on top of the cabbage rolls. Now pour on the olive oil. Add enough water to cover the rolls and put a heavy plate upside down on top of them. Bring to the boil, and simmer, covered, for 45 minutes.

This can be eaten hot, but it is considered at its best when left to stand and eaten cold. (Note in this context, absence of meat and the use of oil instead of butter.)

Stuffed vine leaves

There is absolutely no reason why you shouldn't achieve something far more interesting than those insipid little green rolls you can buy in tins. Even if you don't know someone with a grape vine, the leaves are now widely available, preserved in brine, either in packets or in tins.

If you can find fresh vine leaves, blanch them in boiling water, just enough to make them pliable, and then drain. If you are using the preserved ones, take them out of the packet or tin, rinse them, and pour boiling water over them in a bowl. Leave for about 20 minutes. Drain them in a colander and put them in cold water for 3 minutes. This process will de-salinate them.

The very small rolls are made with young vine leaves and are usually served cold as part of a mezé. Larger 'packets' can be eaten like other stuffed vegetables . . . with a knife and fork. You can pick up the little ones, served cold, in your fingers.

Koupepia

'Little cigars'
Cyprus

30 vine leaves
1 medium onion, finely
  chopped
2 tablespoons olive oil
350 g/12 oz finely minced
  lamb (or a mixture of lamb
  and veal or even veal and
  pork)
100 g/4 oz short-grain rice,
  washed and drained

1 tablespoon parsley, finely
  chopped
1 teaspoon mint, finely
  chopped
salt and freshly ground pepper

to cover:
2 tablespoons olive oil
lemon juice
stock or water

Cook the onion in the oil until soft. Mix with all the other filling
ingredients.

Lay a vine leaf shiny side down. Snip off the stem. Put 1
tablespoon of filling near the stem end. Fold the stem end over and
then fold the sides towards the middle. Roll up firmly.

Line the bottom of a heavy pan with vine leaves. Now arrange the
little cigars on top, close together, in layers. Cover with a few more
vine leaves. Now pour over the olive oil. Then add just enough stock
or water, mixed with 1 to 2 tablespoons lemon juice, to cover. Put
a heavy plate upside down on top. Bring to boil and simmer very
slowly, covered, for 1 hour.

Koupepia can be eaten hot with an *avgolemono* sauce (see page
158). But, despite the meat filling, they are often eaten cold,
sometimes accompanied by a bowl of yogurt.

For those who prefer a meatless filling, here are some other
suggestions. These meatless fillings can, of course, be eaten hot, if
you like.

First of all you could substitute 225 g/8 oz mushrooms, finely
chopped and lightly sautéed with the onion, for the meat in the
above recipe.

A very simple filling consists merely of the substitution of a
bunch of spring onions for the onion and meat. In this case, please
use pure virgin olive oil, as you will have a chance to appreciate its
flavour. (I do this with many dishes to be served cold, though it is
more expensive. See oil, page 183.)

In place of the meat, you could use 2 tablespoons raisins, or 2 tablespoons pine nuts and 1 tablespoon raisins, omitting the mint.

Individual vegetables

Vegetables are not cooked singly to the extent that they are in Britain, but some Middle Eastern recipes for individual vegetables now follow, listed here in (English) alphabetical order.

Artichokes

Despite their name, Jerusalem artichokes (which have a delicious flavour but are hell to clean) are not popular in the Middle East, though they do exist. Some suggest that the English name is a corruption of girasol – sunflower – and really has nothing to do with the city at all. What is generally meant by 'artichokes' is the globe or leafy variety.

In England, these are normally boiled. Then the leaves are peeled off one by one, and their tips dipped in melted butter or vinaigrette. Finally the fluffy, aptly named 'choke' is removed and the heart (base) eaten with the butter or dressing. Some people say that all this effort – and debris – is not worth while for the small result, in terms of quantity. I don't agree, but there *are* other ways to enjoy artichokes. In Cyprus, the hearts are crunched up raw, with a squeeze of lemon juice. I think this is almost as bad as crunching a raw potato, but Cypriot friends rave about the flavour.

Artichokes are in season in Britain for quite a short time and are not cheap. However, they are one of the few vegetables which retain quite a lot of their quality when tinned. Both the recipes that follow can be made with tinned artichoke hearts, but I must stress than this is second-best.

—————— *Anginares ala polita* ——————

Braised artichokes
Greece

This is a spring recipe, with tiny fresh vegetables accompanying the artichokes.

12 globe artichokes *or* 12
  tinned artichoke hearts
(for preparing fresh artichokes,
  you will need a lemon, flour
  and salted water)
1 bunch of spring onions,
  including half the green
  stems, chopped
12 button onions, peeled
  (optional)

12 baby carrots, scraped
12 new potatoes, scraped
salt and freshly ground black
  pepper
2 tablespoons dill, chopped

to cover:
chicken stock or water
150 ml/¼ pint olive oil
the juice of a lemon

If you are using fresh artichokes, prepare them as follows: cut off
the stem just below the base. Remove the tough outer leaves. Trim
3 cm/1¼ inches off the tops of the inner leaves with kitchen
scissors. Now, with a spoon, scoop out the purple inmost leaves and
the fluffy choke that lies beneath. (Do this carefully: you should get
rid of all the choke but not remove any of the precious heart.)

As each artichoke is prepared, rub it over with a squeezed lemon
and drop it into a bowl containing water stirred with the juice of the
lemon, 2 tablespoons flour and a little salt. (This is to prevent
discoloration.)

If you are using tinned artichokes, rinse them in a colander.

Line a large, shallow pan with the chopped spring onion. On top,
put the whole onions (if used), the carrots, new potatoes and
artichokes. Season to taste and sprinkle with the dill. Pour on the
olive oil. Add just enough stock or water to cover, and the lemon
juice. Cover with a lid and cook very gently for about 30 minutes.
Arrange the cooked vegetables attractively on a dish and pour the
liquid over them.

This is usually eaten tepid or cold, but not chilled. If you want it
hot, do let it stand for at least 5 minutes, so that the oil 'melds' with
the liquid in the sauce.

Note: Some people like this sauce to be thickened with 2 teaspoons
of flour or cornflour mixed with a little cold water. This is added to
the liquid in the pan after the vegetables have been removed and
cooked for at least 1 minute. With a growing dislike of flour-based
sauces (see *avgolemono*, page 158) I'm against this.

Anginares me avgolemono

Artichokes with egg and lemon sauce
Greece

I note here that artichokes are often served in Greece with an *avgolemono* sauce. In this case, prepare the artichokes as for the previous recipe. Then cook them in boiling salted water, to which you have added a good squeeze of lemon juice and a tablespoon of olive oil, for about 30 minutes. Serve with *avgolemono* (see page 158) and garnish with chopped parsley or a little chopped dill.

Anginares me Koukia

Artichokes with broad beans
Cyprus

This dish is also prepared in Greece, but the Cyprus version uses garlic instead of spring onions and *rigani* (oregano) instead of dill.

6 artichoke hearts, preferably
    fresh, but you can use tinned
    ones
the juice of 2 lemons
3 tablespoons olive oil
2 cloves of garlic, crushed

1 tablespoon *rigani* (oregano)
salt and freshly ground black
    pepper
675 g/1½ lb young broad
    beans, shelled

Prepare the artichokes as for *Anginares ala polita* (see page 93), but discard all the leaves and just use the hearts (bases). When they are prepared, put them in a large pan with the lemon juice, oil, garlic, oregano and seasonings. Cover with water, bring to the boil, and cook for 10 minutes. Add the broad beans, reduce the heat, and cook very slowly (you should not need to add more water) for 20 minutes. Serve hot (after letting them stand for 5 minutes), warm or cold.

Note: As with *Anginares ala polita*, you may like to add flour or cornflour. Again, I am opposed.

Aubergines

In Turkey the aubergine has been described as 'the sultan among vegetables'. I look back with melancholy to comparatively recent times when it was practically unknown in Britain. Those days are over, though I doubt if even today you will find many displays like those seen in the Limassol market all through the summer: long thin purple ones, giant blue-black ones and the small pure white ones (they are rarer) that gave rise to the name 'eggplant'.

In the Cyprus climate, aubergines grow with rapid fertility. We have a large flower-bed at the back of our courtyard. One year – soon after our arrival – we planted aubergines there. The result, in a few weeks, was a dense 'Sleeping Beauty' thicket, hung with uncountable 'fruits'. We almost became tired of aubergines that year!

Here are four recipes that illustrate the aubergine's dominant qualities.

Imam bayildi

The Imam fainted
Turkey

Why did the Imam swoon at this dish? Because of its extravagant use of olive oil? (Imams are said to be parsimonious.) Because he ate so much of it that he passed out? Or from sheer ecstasy at its deliciousness? All these explanations have been suggested.

Although everyone uses the Turkish name for it, other nations stake claims to the dish. The Armenians and the Kurds both say they originated it. So do the Greeks, who explain that a Greek cook prepared it for an Imam. (It has always been part of Greek cuisine.) However, here, I tentatively attribute it to Turkey because of its name, and as a friendly gesture from a Hellenophile.

8 long, medium-size aubergines
200 ml/7 fl oz olive oil
2 large onions, finely sliced
2 green peppers, seeded and finely sliced
4 cloves of garlic (you can use less), finely chopped
3 medium-size tomatoes, peeled, seeded and chopped

2 tablespoons parsley, finely chopped
1 teaspoon allspice (optional)
salt and freshly ground black pepper
150 ml/¼ pint water, with juice of a lemon

garnish:
1 tablespoon parsley, finely chopped

Cut a deep slit lengthwise down each aubergine, stopping short of top and base. Some people also take off little strips of peel to create a striped effects, but many – including me – don't. Place the aubergines in a bowl of very salty water for 30 minutes. Meanwhile, you can prepare the filling. Drain the aubergines, gently squeeze out moisture with your hands, and dry with paper towels.

In a heavy pan, heat half the olive oil. Gently fry the onions with the green peppers and garlic until soft. Then combine them with the tomatoes, parsley, allspice (if used) and salt and black pepper to taste.

Now put the rest of the olive oil in the pan, and fry the aubergines, gently turning several times (take care not to spoil the shape), until they begin to soften. Take the pan off the heat, and turn all the aubergines so the slit is facing upwards. If you prefer to bake them in the oven, you can transfer them to an ovenproof dish. Force as much filling as possible into the slits, and put any that is left on top. Pour on the water and lemon juice. Either cook on top of the stove at very gentle heat, or bake in the oven, preheated to 160°C/325°F/gas 3, for 45 minutes. Leave to cool at room temperature. Then chill, if you like. This dish is at its best eaten cool or cold and garnished with parsley.

Melitzanes sto fourno

Aubergines cooked in the oven
Cyprus

This is our friend Mrs Rebecca Savvides' family recipe.

About 1 kg/2¼ lb aubergines
the juice of ½ lemon
1 kg/2¼ lb ripe tomatoes,
  peeled and diced
1 onion, grated
2 cloves of garlic, crushed
  (optional)

225 g/8 oz Feta cheese, grated
  (you can use another cheese
  of your choice)
100 to 150 ml/4 to 6 fl oz
  olive oil
salt and freshly ground black
  pepper

Peel the aubergines and slice them into rounds. Put them in salted water with the lemon juice for at least 10 minutes. Remove and drain. Mix the tomatoes onion and cheese and the crushed garlic, if used, together, seasoning them with pepper and salt (but be careful with the salt if you are using Feta, as it is very salty). Now lightly oil a casserole. Put in a layer of aubergines, then one of the tomato mixture, using up the ingredients till you end with the tomato mixture on top. As you go, sprinkle olive oil on each layer. Cook in the oven preheated to 200°C/400°F/gas 5 for between 1 and 1½ hours, covered with a lid or with foil for the first two-thirds of cooking time. Remove the covering for the last 20 or 30 minutes, to brown.

Moussaka horis kreas

Meatless moussaka
Greece

If you compare this recipe with the recipe for moussaka with meat (see page 140), you will see that the main difference lies in doubling the quantities of aubergines and omitting the lamb.

1 kg/2¼ lb aubergines
2 medium onions, finely
  chopped
100 ml/4 fl oz olive oil
2 large ripe tomatoes, peeled
  and diced
1 tablespoon parsley, finely
  chopped
salt and freshly ground black
  pepper

sauce
300 ml/½ pint milk
the yolks of 2 large eggs
salt and freshly ground black
  pepper
a pinch of cinnamon

Slice half the aubergines, salt them, and leave them in a colander to drain for 30 minutes.

Meanwhile, cook the remaining aubergines in boiling, salted water until soft. Allow them to cool, then peel them. Soften the onions in half the oil. Mash the boiled aubergines and mix them with the onions and oil, the tomatoes and parsley.

Squeeze the salted aubergine slices gently, to remove excess moisture. Wash them in cold water and dry them. Fry them in the remaining oil, turning once, till golden. Oil a deep baking dish. Put in alternate layers of the sliced aubergines and the aubergine and tomato mixture, topping with aubergine slices. Mix your sauce ingredients, beating with a fork or whisk. Pour them over the aubergines and bake at 180°C/350°F/gas 4 till a golden crust has formed. This is good hot or cold.

Hunkar beyendi

Sultan's delight
Turkey

One cookery writer whom I usually much admire says that this dish should be 'lumpy'. However, the consensus is that it was its creamy refinement that so delighted the sultan, and having tried both methods, I agree with the latter view.

1 kg/2¼ lb aubergines	salt
the juice of ½ lemon	50 g/2 oz cheese, grated (I
100 g/4 oz butter	recommend half Parmesan,
100 g/4 oz flour	half Gruyère, even though
575 ml/1 pint milk	these are foreign cheeses)

The skins of the aubergines must be blackened before peeling, as the smoky taste is an important element in the dish. Put each over a flame (the gas flame of a cooker will do), holding it on a long fork, or put them under a grill, or on an electric hotplate, or, as a last resort, in a red-hot oven, until the skins have charred and the aubergines feel soft when prodded with a fork. Peel the skin off thoroughly.

Cover the peeled aubergines with water into which you have

squeezed the lemon juice. Leave for about 20 minutes.

Make a roux with the butter, flour and salt, cooking thoroughly to get rid of the taste of the large quantity of uncooked flour. Gradually blend in the milk, stirring constantly. Season with salt to taste. You can add a little white pepper, which I never normally recommend, but this dish should look very pale.

Now drain the aubergines, squeezing out as much moisture as possible. Mash them, gradually adding the sauce when they are smooth. (I do this in the food processor, with, first, a little of the sauce, to moisten; then I add the rest.) Now put the mixture in a saucepan, and stir in the grated cheese till melted. Put in a serving dish, and garnish with parsley if you wish.

Hot (as I like it), this traditionally forms an accompaniment to *Tas kebabi* (see page 135), but you can serve it with other stews or with grilled meat or chicken. Some eat it cold, but the butter and flour spoil this for me.

Broad beans

Full of flavour when young and tender (as opposed to old and tough), it always seems to me a waste to dry them. The Greeks fry the very young ones – whole.

Koukia tiganita

Fried broad beans
Greece

450 g/1 lb very young broad
   beans in their pods
flour for coating, seasoned
   with salt and freshly ground
   black pepper
olive oil for frying

to accompany:
lemon wedges

Wash the beans, and remove any strings with the tops and tails. Do not shell. Drop them into boiling, salted water and cook rapidly for 5 minutes. Drain and pat dry.

Roll the bean pods in seasoned flour. Shallow fry in very hot olive oil until golden brown, turning. Serve at once, with lemon to squeeze over them.

For shelled broad beans, see *Anginares me koukia* (page 94).

Courgettes

I find these a bit insipid. Some people use them instead of aubergines in a moussaka, but this is not traditional. Eggs and spices can brighten them up (see *Kousa ma' bayd bil-furn*, page 46) but if you are going to cook them plain, I advise against boiling. Fry them in olive oil, just as they are, or dipped in egg.

The following recipe certainly adds interest.

—————— Kousa bi-tahina ——————

Baked courgettes in tahini
Lebanon

2 large onions, chopped
3 tablespoons olive oil
50 g/2 oz pine nuts
675 g/1½ lb courgettes,
    washed, drained and cut into
    rounds 6 mm/¼ inch thick

4 tablespoons tahini
4 tablespoons lemon juice
3 cloves of garlic, crushed
1 teaspoon salt
½ teaspoon allspice

Soften the onions in half the olive oil. Just before they are done, add the pine nuts. In the rest of the oil brown the courgette rounds. Line the bottom of an oiled casserole with a layer of courgettes, then one of onion and pine nuts, finishing with a layer of courgettes. Mix the tahini with the lemon juice, garlic, salt and allspice. Add water and beat till you have a smooth thin cream. Pour this over the mixture in the casserole and bake at 180°C/350°F/gas 4 until the top is browned.

Kolokythia keftedes

Courgette rissoles
Greece

675 g/1½ lb courgettes *or*
  marrow (provided it isn't old
  and stringy)
2 slices stale white bread
2 onions, minced
1 beaten egg
100 g/4 oz Kefalotiri or
  Parmesan, finely grated

1 tablespoon parsley, finely
  chopped
½ teaspoon dried mint,
  powdered
flour for coating
olive oil for frying

Peel the courgettes or marrow. If you use marrow, remove the large seeds. Boil until tender in salted water.

Cut the crusts off the bread and soak it in a little water for 1 to 2 minutes. Then squeeze the liquid out. Mash the marrow and mix it with the other ingredients or put the whole lot in the food processor, whizzing for 30 seconds.

Form into small rissoles. Roll them in flour and fry them in hot olive oil until golden. Eat hot – with a squeeze of lemon juice, if you like.

Leeks

Beautiful leeks sometimes appear in the Limassol market, but no Cypriot seems to cook them, and it has been said here that 'Leeks are eaten ... by the English'. This is not the case in Greece or in other parts of the Middle East.

I am sorry not to give cooked leeks a recipe all of their own (except as a salad, on page 120), but I give instructions for using them as an alternative to spinach (see *Prassorizo*, page 105 and *Prassopitta*, page 107). They are also a very popular filling for an *eggah* (see page 47).

Okra

Bamies Yahni

Okra stew
Cyprus

Bamies are sometimes called 'ladies' fingers', but are most widely known as okra, which you can now sometimes obtain in England. They are always available tinned, but I don't recommend them.

The *bamies* are sometimes cooked with meat, in the manner of *fassolakia* (French beans) on page 134. But I like them best very simply cooked with oil and tomatoes.

1 kg/2¼ lb okra
200 ml/7 fl oz olive oil
2 large onions, chopped
   vertically into 'wings'
450 g/1 lb tomatoes, peeled
   and chopped
1 teaspoon salt

optional:
1 stock cube, 2 cloves of garlic,
   crushed, a sprinkling of
   parsley as a garnish

Buy only small fresh-looking okra. Clean them thoroughly, removing stalks and trimming round the 'caps'. Now, in Cyprus, we would put them on a cloth on a tray in the sun for ten minutes, but that could be a problem in England! You could put them in a warm oven for a minute or two to dry.

Heat the oil in a small pan. Sauter a few okra at a time, removing them and setting them aside as soon as they start to brown. Now cook the onions (with the garlic, if used) in the oil until golden. Put the onions and oil, the tomatoes, salt, a stock cube (if you share many Cypriot cooks' passion for them), with 200 ml/7 fl oz cold water. Bring to boil, then simmer very slowly on low heat for 30 minutes. They are delicious hot – left to stand for a few minutes – or cold. I like to sprinkle on a little parsley.

Potatoes

Latecomers to the Middle Eastern scene, potatoes will never aspire to the place occupied by rice and burghul, or play the role they do in Northern Europe and in all English-speaking countries. I must note here, however, that in Cyprus today, chips are ubiquitous, and it would be a great mistake to suppose that they are cooked only for the benefit of tourists; they have become a national dish.

Potatoes are generally treated as just another vegetable – for which there are some interesting recipes.

Batata mahshiyeh

Stuffed potatoes
Lebanon

One would think that a thoroughly washed potato was a natural for stuffing – the perfect container being provided by its skin. This is not the case in the Middle East where stuffed potatoes are always peeled.

12 fairly large potatoes (they should be all the same size), peeled, washed and patted dry
75 g/3 oz butter
2 medium onions, finely chopped
450 g/1 lb minced lamb
about 1 tablespoon olive oil
1 tablespoon tomato paste

100 g/4 oz pine nuts or chopped walnuts
½ teaspoon allspice
salt and freshly ground black pepper

to cover:
2 tablespoons tomato paste
2 cloves of garlic, crushed
450 ml/¾ pint water

Carefully 'core' each potato with an apple-corer, but don't pierce the far end. Your hollow should not be too big or the potato will break. Melt the butter in a large pan, and lightly fry the potatoes in it for a few minutes, turning them till they take on colour. Set aside.

In the same pan, cook the onion and lamb in just enough oil to prevent them sticking. Stir in the remaining ingredients a few minutes before the onion and meat are cooked through. Use the mixture to fill the hollows in the potatoes.

Put the stuffed potatoes in a lightly oiled fireproof dish. Now mix the tomato paste, garlic and water. Season, and reduce over high heat for 5 minutes. Pour over the potatoes and bake at 200°C/400°F/gas 6 for up to 1 hour until the potatoes are tender. (Check that the potatoes aren't falling apart!)

Batata bil-toum

Potatoes with garlic
Lebanon

1 kg/2¼ lb new potatoes, scraped
75 ml/3 fl oz olive oil
4 cloves of garlic, crushed
salt
freshly ground black pepper
½ teaspoon ground cumin
½ teaspoon ground coriander
a handful of fresh coriander leaves, chopped (optional)

Quickly fry the potatoes in the olive oil until golden. Add all the other ingredients, except the coriander leaves, if used. Just cover with water, and simmer until the potatoes are cooked … only a few minutes.

You can garnish with fresh coriander, if you want to. I hate the taste and (untraditionally) substitute parsley.

Note: For another way of cooking new potatoes, see *Afelia* (page 109).

Patata keftedes

Potato rissoles
Greece

675 g/1½ lb potatoes
25 g/1 oz butter
salt and freshly ground black pepper
2 eggs, beaten
1 tablespoon parsley, finely chopped
2 spring onions, minced or grated
75 g/3 oz cheese, grated (optional)
flour for coating
olive oil for frying

Peel, boil and mash the potatoes with the butter, salt and pepper. Add the eggs, parsley, spring onions and cheese, if used. Mix together lightly, and form into little round flat cakes. Coat with flour, and fry in very hot olive oil until crisp and golden brown. Even the Greeks eat these hot!

Spinach

Spanakorizo

Spinach with rice
Greece

1 kg/2¼ lb spinach	1 tablespoon parsley, chopped
150 ml/¼ pint olive oil	the juice of 1 large or 2 small
a bunch of spring onions,	lemons
chopped	salt and freshly ground black
175 g/6 oz short-grain rice	pepper
1½ teaspoons dill, chopped	450 ml/¾ pint water

Wash the spinach thoroughly, removing discoloured or damaged leaves, and tough ribs. Shred the leaves and chop the tender stalks.

Now heat the olive oil in a heavy saucepan, and cook the onions until soft. Add the washed, drained rice and cook rapidly, stirring all the time, for 3 minutes. Add the rest of the ingredients, including the water, which should be boiling. Bring to the boil and add the spinach. Stir, cover, and simmer very slowly for 15 minutes. Remove from the heat, cover with a cloth and put the lid on your pan. Leave to stand for 10 minutes, when all the liquid should have been absorbed.

Note: Some people make this into more of a pilafi, by using up to 450 g/1 lb rice, and adjusting the liquid accordingly.

Variation: Prassorizo
        Leeks with rice

Replace the spinach with the white parts of 8 leeks cut into 5 cm/2 inch pieces. Omit the spring onions and replace the dill with a good pinch of cinnamon. Soften the pieces of leek in the olive oil, and proceed as above.

Spanakopitta

Spinach pie
Greece and Cyprus

I give two versions of this famous spinach and cheese pie. But let me first admit to you that I never make my own pastry. It is lucky for me that I live in the Middle East, as really only professional confectioners make their own filo (*yufka* to the Turks), the pastry chiefly used in cookery. All experts admit that it is extraordinarily difficult to make, and most don't advise it. The very best cooks buy their filo from shops. You can now do this all over London, in most large towns and in other places. (Any Cypriot should be able to tell you.)

Filo is remarkably easy to deal with. Take the number of sheets you need out of the packet. Replace the rest, wrap the packet in foil, and put it in the refrigerator, where the filo will keep for up to 2 weeks. (It must never be allowed to dry out. While working with it, you should keep the sheets you are not yet using covered with a cloth wrung out in cold water.)

I now turn to the other form of pastry chiefly used in Middle Eastern cookery: 'puff'. I use commercial puff pastry. Many Cypriots do. The 'Jus-rol' brand is stocked by even the smallest grocers, and this works well for *Purdah Pilau* (see page 154).

Of the two versions of *spanakopitta* I give here, I prefer the first, made with filo and without a rich *béchamel* sauce. The second, which I learnt from our friend Androula Costi, is a more modern and opulent version.

Spanakopitta I

1 kg/2¼ lb spinach
the juice of ½ lemon
100 ml/4 oz olive oil
1 large onion, chopped
1 bunch spring onions,
  chopped
3 tablespoons parsley, chopped
½ teaspoon ground nutmeg
2 teaspoons dill or fennel,
  chopped (optional)

225 g/8 oz grated cheese (Feta is traditional, but you can use Cheddar: whichever you use, I would advise that 50 g/2 oz of the total is Kefalotiri or Parmesan)
3 to 4 eggs, lightly beaten
salt and freshly ground black pepper
10 sheets filo pastry
melted butter for brushing the pastry

Wash the spinach thoroughly. Cut off tough stems. Chop tender stalks finely and shred leaves. Put into a large pan of boiling salted water with the juice of half a lemon, and boil for 10 minutes. Drain thoroughly. After draining, squeeze out any excess moisture with your hands.

Heat the olive oil, and fry the onion until soft, adding the spring onions for the last third of frying time. Now add the drained spinach with all the other ingredients and stir. If using Feta, check the saltiness before seasoning.

Brush a 25 × 30 cm/10 × 12 inch baking dish with melted butter. Line it with 5 sheets of filo, brushing melted butter between each. Spread the sheets around so that there are no gaps, and a bit hangs over the edge. (Overlapping sheets don't matter.) Now spread the spinach mixture out over the pastry base. Top with the remaining 5 sheets of filo, again brushing each sheet with melted butter. Tuck in the edges, trimming a little off if necessary.

Brush the top lightly with butter and, using a sharp knife, mark it into the large squares into which it is traditionally cut. Finally, brush over with a little cold water. Bake at 190°C/375°F/gas 5 for 45 minutes: the pie should be puffed and golden. Leave it to stand for 10 minutes before serving. I like this pie better hot, but it's good cold, too.

Variation: Prassopitta
        Leek pie

Replace the spinach with an equal quantity of leeks. Use only the white parts, boiled in salted water until soft, drained and then shredded. Omit the onions and all but 2 teaspoons of olive oil, which should be mixed with the cooked leeks and other ingredients. Omit the dill or fennel.

Spanakopitta II

With my increasing dislike of the *béchamel* and other flour-based sauces, combined with the fact that I don't advise using filo for this recipe (because the sauce makes it soggy), I can't wax as enthusiastic about this version as I do about the other, though many Cypriots prefer it.

1 kg/2¼ lb spinach
the juice of ½ a lemon
375 g/13 oz 'Jus-rol' or other
   puff pastry
melted butter

for the sauce:
40 g/1½ oz butter
40 g/1½ oz flour

600 ml/1 pint milk
salt and freshly ground black
   pepper
225 g/8 oz grated Haloumi
   (you can use Cheddar or
   other cheese)
½ teaspoon cinnamon
4 eggs, lightly beaten

Prepare, boil and drain the spinach as for *Spanakopitta I*. Make the sauce, adding cheese and cinnamon. Take it off the stove and, after a moment, mix in the beaten eggs. Incorporate the thoroughly drained spinach, stirring it in with a wooden spoon.

Butter a baking-dish as for *Spanakopitta I*. Line it with half the rolled-out puff pastry. Spoon and spread the mixture on top. Cover with the rest of the pastry. Mark into squares, brush with butter mixed with a little water and bake as for *Spanakopitta I*.

Even though puff pastry is used instead of filo, this version seems to me soggy if eaten cold.

Afelia

Cyprus

This is an exclusively Cypriot contribution to cookery, making interesting use of the coriander seeds which are so popular. Here, three vegetables are cooked in this way: artichokes, mushrooms and potatoes. (See page 137 for a meat recipe.)

50 ml/2 fl oz olive oil
100 ml/4 fl oz dry red wine
salt and freshly ground black
   pepper

1 tablespoon coriander seeds,
   roughly crushed

Anginares

Artichokes

Prepare 6 artichokes as for *Anginares ala polita* (page 92). Then cut each into quarters. Fry in oil until lightly browned. Reduce the heat. Add wine and seasonings, and cook for 5 minutes. Add the coriander seeds for the last 2 minutes.

Manitaria

Mushrooms

Trim 225 g/8 oz medium sized mushrooms and wipe them with a cloth. (I believe that one should hardly ever wash mushrooms, let alone peel them.) Fry them in the oil till brown. Add the wine and seasonings. Cook for 10 minutes, adding the coriander seeds for the last 2 minutes.

Patates

Potatoes

450 g/1 lb small new potatoes: wash and dry them. Then crack each one with a sharp blow from a wooden mallet or pestle. Heat the oil and brown the potatoes rapidly, shaking the pan. Reduce the heat and add the wine and seasonings. Simmer covered over low heat for about 15 minutes, adding the coriander seed 2 minutes before the end of the cooking time.

SALADS

The salads here seem to fall into two categories: those containing grains or pulses, some of which seem exciting and unusual to Western cooks, and those made more conventionally with raw or, in a few cases, cooked vegetables.

Grains and pulses

Fattoush

Salad with bread
Lebanon

This provides you with a first-class opportunity to say that my first choice contains neither grain nor pulse. But the pieces of Arab bread included in this salad (which make it instantly recognizable to the novice) are of course made of . . . flour.

Fattoush also gives me a chance to illustrate some of the problems involved in research into Middle Eastern cuisine. I give 2 recipes.

The first is that of a brilliant cook, Soraya Antonius:

'tomato
cucumbers
cos lettuce
onions and/or spring onions
parsley
mint
purslane

sweet pepper (optional)
lemons or sour pomegranate
    juice *or* sumac
toasted Arab bread (not pitta)
olive oil
salt

'This is a traditional accompaniment to *Mujaddara* (see page 80) and is a pleasant salad to go with grilled shellfish served cold. The respective quantities are not really important, provided they balance each other agreeably and the bread is only one ingredient among many; but it isn't *fattoush* without purslane.

'Break the toast into pieces about the size of a large man's thumbnail and leave to soak in lemon or other juice while preparing the rest of the ingredients. Then add everything else: cucumbers, peeled and diced, the lettuce shredded, the mint, parsley and onions chopped finely, tomato peeled and chopped roughly after seeding, purslane leaves whole but without the stalks, and the sweet pepper if used (it doesn't add much) seeded and chopped. Add salt and olive oil, mix and correct seasoning if necessary. Serve immediately.'

Prepared by Soraya, this salad is indeed magical, but I must admit that her recipe makes even me – an experienced cook – a little nervous. I would feel unkind if I presented it to a learner or to someone with no experience of Middle Eastern cookery. So I have given a second recipe: a rough and inferior guide for those who ask, 'But *how much* cucumber?' as I believe most of us do.

As I note elsewhere (see page 116), purslane is not easy to find in Britain nowadays, which might seem to preclude the making of *fattoush*. Though they stress its good qualities in this salad, there are Middle Eastern cooks who do not consider purslane essential. Accordingly, in the recipe that follows, purslane is optional.

1 round of Arab bread
2 tablespoons lemon juice *or* pomegranate juice
1 lettuce heart, shredded
1 medium cucumber, peeled and diced
2 medium tomatoes, peeled, seeded and chopped
4 spring onions, finely chopped

the leaves of 1 bunch purslane, if possible
1 green pepper, seeded and finely chopped
4 tablespoons parsley, chopped
2 tablespoons fresh mint, finely chopped
salt
olive oil

Toast the Arab bread under a hot grill till crisp and golden. Break it into small pieces and put these aside to soak in the lemon or sour pomegranate juice. Prepare all the other ingredients, and then mix them well with the bread. Season with salt and dress with oil. You may need a little lemon juice at this stage, despite having soaked the bread in juice.

Tabbouleh

Burghul and parsley salad
Lebanon

Though the Syrians and Jordanians also lay claim to this, the Lebanese consider it their national salad, and their mastery of it is acknowledged.

As always, there will be disagreements, especially about the proportions of burghul, parsley and tomatoes.

100 g/4 oz fine burghul

1 bunch spring onions, chopped

2 firm but ripe medium tomatoes, peeled, seeded and chopped

100 g/4 oz parsley, finely chopped

4 tablespoons fresh mint, chopped

2 tablespoons lemon juice

3 tablespoons virgin olive oil

salt and freshly ground black pepper to taste

a pinch of cayenne (optional)

$\frac{1}{2}$ teaspoon cinnamon (optional)

Wash the fine burghul and leave it to soak in cold water for 30 minutes. Then drain it thoroughly and squeeze out excess moisture with your hands. You can now spread the burghul on a cloth to dry still more, for 15 minutes, if you want to.

Mix the chopped onions and tomatoes well with the burghul. Now mix the parsley and mint in with the burghul. Dress with the remaining ingredients, which should have been mixed together well.

Traditionally, this salad is scooped up, using crisp young lettuce leaves, vine leaves or very young cabbage leaves.

Note: Unusually for a Lebanese recipe, this one specifies more olive oil than lemon juice. Some people add extra lemon juice (served, mixed with a little salt, in a jug) at the table.

Bazergan

Burghul salad
Syria

This salad (also claimed by the Assyrians) is from outside 'my' parts of the Middle East, but it dazzled me at Prue Seymour's Easter picnic (see page 85).

225 g/8 oz fine burghul
6 tablespoons olive oil
1 large onion, finely chopped
1 teaspoon oregano
4 tablespoons parsley, finely
chopped
3 tablespoons walnuts, finely
chopped (an innovative
friend of mine substituted
pecan nuts)

2 tablespoons lemon juice or
pomegranate juice (see page
184)
1 teaspoon ground cumin
1 teaspoon ground coriander
½ teaspoon allspice

Prepare the burghul as for *Tabbouleh* (see opposite). Heat the oil
and use it to soften the onion. Add the onion and oil to the burghul.
Now mix in all the other ingredients. Allow to stand. Serve chilled,
heaped on a serving dish. Very pretty – and delicious.

Piyaz

White bean salad
Turkey

225 g/8 oz dried white haricot
beans
1 clove of garlic, crushed
1 small onion, thinly sliced
4 tablespoons olive oil
the juice of half a lemon
1 small green pepper, thinly
sliced

garnish:
3 hard-boiled eggs
1 tablespoon parsley, chopped
4 stoned black olives
1 tomato, peeled and thinly
sliced

Soak the beans overnight. Boil and then simmer them until tender
but still firm. Drain, and add the other ingredients to the beans
while they are still hot, mixing gently but well.

As far as the garnish is concerned, take your choice. You could
use them all. I particularly favour the parsley, mixed in after the
beans have cooled, and the quartered hard-boiled eggs.

Salatit loubia hmra

Kidney bean salad
Lebanon

Kidney beans look so pretty that I was delighted to come across this nice Lebanese salad.

225 g/8 oz red kidney beans
1 green pepper, seeded and chopped
2 tablespoons spring onions, chopped

1 tablespoon parsley, chopped
2 tablespoons olive oil
the juice of 1 lemon
salt and freshly ground pepper
lettuce leaves

Put the beans into a saucepan with 575 ml/1 pint water. Cover them and bring them to the boil. Simmer for a few minutes. Then let them stand for 2 hours, before bringing them to the boil again, and simmering for 1 hour. Drain off any remaining liquid.

When the beans have cooled, stir in the green pepper, spring onion and parsley. Mix the oil, lemon juice and seasoning. Line a salad bowl with lettuce leaves and arrange the beans in it. Pour the dressing over them.

Salatit ades

Lentil salad
Egypt

225 g/8 oz brown lentils
oil and lemon dressing (see page 162)
2 tablespoons parsley, chopped
2 cloves of garlic, crushed (optional)

1 medium onion, thinly sliced
1 ripe medium tomato, peeled and chopped

Wash the lentils and cook them, simmering at low heat for 1 hour, after bringing to the boil. Drain them, and while they are still warm, dress with the oil and lemon mixture. When they have cooled stir in the other ingredients, mixing well.

Rice salad

I have always been fond of this alternative to the perpetual potato salad, and have often made it in Cyprus; the Middle East provides suitable ingredients in abundance. Yet, talking to Middle Easterners and consulting culinary authorities, I can't find a traditional rice salad.

Why do I include it? This is a very conservative part of the world in culinary terms. But when the ingredients and style of a dish are well suited to an environment and would fit easily into its culinary pattern, one should dare to innovate.

Therefore, I prepare rice according to Method 1 (see page 63) or 2 (see page 64), using oil instead of butter. While it is still warm, I add oil and lemon dressing (see page 162). When it has cooled, I add, according to my mood, from the following:

tomatoes, peeled, seeded and
   finely chopped
cucumbers, diced
parsley, finely chopped
mint, chopped
black and green olives, stoned
   and chopped
onions or spring onions, finely
   chopped

capers, chopped
green peppers, finely chopped
powdered cumin, coriander,
   allspice
salt and freshly ground black
   pepper

Green and vegetable salads

An interesting assortment of green herbs features strongly in Arab salads. Apart from lettuce and cabbage, fresh coriander, rocket, purslane and parsley make contributions in their own right.

Fresh coriander
As far as I can discover, you either love the flavour or loathe it. I find that it adds the taste of soap to whatever it appears in. (The seeds, crushed or ground – see *Afelia*, page 137, and other recipes – are an entirely different experience.) In summer, you can find fresh coriander in many foreign provision stores (its Indian name is *dhaniya*). It looks very like the flat-leafed Mediterranean parsley

(see below) except that the stems are coarse and knotted together. (In a hurry, at the market, I have mistaken it for parsley, and not discovered my error till unwrapping, and its – to me – unpleasant aroma wafted up.) Experiment for yourself. You may love it, chopped and added to a salad.

Rocket

Rokka, as it is called in Cyprus, looks rather like spinach, but tastes very like watercress. Some people say it tastes like radishes. Though less popular than coriander, it appears in Cypriot shops in Britain. It adds character to any green salad and has a particular affinity with tomatoes, as has basil. However, though basil grows throughout the Middle East, people never use it for culinary purposes except, occasionally, in pickling.

Purslane

In Cyprus, we call it *glysterida* and the Arabs call it *ba'leh*. It is a small succulent herb with fleshy leaves which rampages, uninvited, over gardens (including our) in summer. It appeared in Britain's first salad recipe in 1393 and was still being cultivated in Victorian kitchen gardens. However, it is seldom found in Britain today, and I can find no mention of it in four modern so-called 'kitchen herbals'. Why not grow your own? Then you can be sure of making a perfect *fattoush* (see page 110), and you can use the leaves in many other salads. The flavour is delicate, the texture unusual and attractive.

Parsley

I suppose that curly British parsley is prettier, but the flat-leafed Mediterranean kind to which I have now become wholly accustomed seems to me to have more flavour. (I often used to buy it in England where you will find it at all sorts of foreign food stores.) For some of the salad recipes in this book, for instance, *tabbouleh*, see page 111, and the recipe that follows now, it seems to me essential. For other recipes where smaller quantities of finely chopped parsley are specified, you can probably use the curly kind. Parsley, you will also notice, is an essential element in Middle Eastern cooking cropping up in recipe after recipe.

Ba'dounis bi-tahina

Parsley with tahini
Lebanon

Illustrating what I have just said about parsley's importance in the Middle East, here is a recipe for a parsley salad.

5 bunches flat-leafed (Mediterranean) parsley	3 tablespoons lemon juice
	3½ tablespoons water
200 g/7 oz tahini	1 clove of garlic, crushed with salt

Pick the leaves off the parsley, when you have washed and dried it. Leave them unchopped. Mix the tahini, lemon juice and water, beating well, and add the garlic. Add another pinch of salt. Put the parsley in a bowl and pour the dressing over it and mix.

The salad is sometimes garnished with slices of hard-boiled egg.

Horiatiki salata

Village salad
Greece and Cyprus

How can I fail to love it, having eaten it all over the Hellenic world for ... yes, more than fifty years?

This is a salad that can vary, though some ingredients must be there. Let me compose a bowl for you, starting with the things you should not omit.

4 ripe tomatoes, cut into wedges (don't peel them)	100 g/4 oz Feta cheese, sliced or broken into pieces
2 small cucumbers (sometimes peeled, sometimes unpeeled, so why not peel one and not the other?) Cut them in half lengthwise, and then slice them vertically, not too thinly	up to a dozen black olives
	salt

All the above must be included, but your salad should also include some of the following:

a handful of flat-leafed parsley, coarsely chopped

1 large mild onion, sliced into rings, or a bunch of spring onions, chopped

1 small Cos lettuce or a small white cabbage, shredded

1 green pepper, seeded and thinly sliced

rocket, purslane or coriander leaves, snipped with scissors

a few chopped capers

a pinch of dill or oregano

a few sprigs of mint

Dress with either oil and lemon or oil and vinegar (see page 163). Bring the salad, beautifully arranged, to the table and toss it there.

Spinach salads

There seem to be no raw spinach salads in this part of the world. The Greeks' cooked-spinach salad does not much appeal to me. They cook tender young leaves for 15 minutes – much too long – in boiling salted water, drain them and dress them with salt, a lot of olive oil and a little lemon juice.

The brilliant Armenians who travel and live all over the Arab world – and there is a large Armenian population in Cyprus – have a much more exciting recipe.

──────────────── *Shomin* ────────────────

Spinach and yogurt salad
Armenia

450 g/1 lb fresh young spinach

1 small onion, finely chopped

2 tablespoons olive oil

salt and freshly ground pepper

300 ml/½ pint yogurt

2 to 3 cloves of garlic, crushed

a sprinkle of paprika

Wash the spinach thoroughly. Cut off the stalks and use only the leaves. Put them in boiling salted water and simmer for 7 to 8 minutes. Drain, then squeeze out any excess moisture with your hands. Chop the spinach finely.

Soften the onion in the oil. Add the chopped spinach and cook for about 5 minutes, stirring. Season with salt and black pepper. Leave to cool.

Mix the yogurt with the garlic. Put the spinach in a bowl, and spoon the yogurt over it. Sprinkle with a little paprika. Some people add an extra garnish of a few chopped walnuts.

Domates salatasi

Tomato salad
Turkey

Simple tomato salads are made all over the Middle East. Very often they consist merely of sliced tomatoes with a spoonful or two of olive oil, salt and black pepper, a little sliced onion and a sprinkling of parsley or some other greenery such as rocket. The Greeks often add a pinch of *rigani* (oregano).

This Turkish salad is only slightly more sophisticated. I like the way the ingredients are decoratively arranged on a plate rather than being all mixed up in a bowl.

4 large firm, ripe tomatoes	salt and freshly ground black
2 thin cucumbers	pepper
50 ml/2 fl oz olive oil	up to 20 black olives
2 tablespoons lemon juice	a good pinch of cumin
a few sprigs of parsley, chopped	

Slice the tomatoes and cucumbers; you can peel them if you want to. On a large plate, arrange 2 rows of sliced tomatoes with a row of cucumber slices down one side of it. Mix the olive oil, lemon juice, parsley and seasoning and pour over the tomatoes and cucumber. Chill for at least an hour. Just before serving, arrange the olives on the opposite side of the plate to the cucumber. Sprinkle the salad with the cumin, and garnish with 2 or 3 sprigs of parsley.

Cucumber with yogurt

Talatouri   Cyprus
Tsatsiki   Greece
Çaçik   Turkey

Everybody claims this cool delicious salad, basically a perfect marriage of 2 ingredients, enlivened with garlic.

575 ml/1 pint thick yogurt
1 large or 2 small cucumbers,
   peeled and finely chopped
2 cloves of garlic, crushed
2 teaspoons dried mint,
   powdered

2 tablespoons olive oil
   (optional)
salt
a sprinkling of cayenne pepper

Mix all together, seasoning to taste. Only in Cyprus do they include olive oil, beating it in to enrich the mixture. Chill before serving.

Note: You can use 1½ tablespoons fresh mint instead of the dried mint, but the latter is preferred in the Middle East.

Leek salad

As a (non-Welsh) campaigner for the leek, I am happy to find it often made into a simple salad in various parts of the Arab world, and including Greece, but not Cyprus.

Thoroughly clean and trim a bunch of young leeks. Put them into boiling, salted water and simmer until tender. Drain them, and dress them with oil and lemon (see page 162). Leave them to cool. Alternatively you can simmer the leeks in 2 tablespoons olive oil, with an equal quantity of water, a squeeze of lemon juice and salt and freshly ground black pepper to taste. Chill and adjust the dressing formed by the cooking liquid, if necessary.

Prepared in either of these ways, a leek salad looks pretty with a sprinkling of parsley and a few black olives scattered over it.

Batata mutabbaleh

Spiced potatoes
Lebanon

A potato salad in the Middle East is often just the same as the ones we're used to. Here is a different cold-potato dish.

6 tablespoons olive oil
225 g/8 oz onions, cut vertically into 'wings'
3 cloves of garlic, finely chopped
50 g/2 oz cooked or tinned chick peas (optional)
1 kg/2¼ lb potatoes peeled and cut into thick slices

450 g/1 lb tomatoes, peeled and chopped (see page 000)
1 tablespoon tomato purée
salt and freshly ground black pepper
1 teaspoon allspice

Heat the oil in a pan and fry the onions and garlic until almost brown. Add the chick peas, if used, and sauter briefly. Add the potatoes and cook, turning them, for about 10 minutes, till they take colour. Mix the tomato and tomato purée, salt, pepper and allspice with enough water to cover the potatoes. Bring to the boil, reduce heat and simmer till the potatoes are tender but not mushy. They will not need draining.

Salata wardiyeh

Pink salad
Lebanon

Leaving *bortsch* apart, I have felt hostile to beetroot for many years. In England it is either savagely pickled in malt vinegar or boiled and tasteless, reminiscent of what used to be called 'salad' in Britain: an old lettuce leaf with a slice of beetroot and a piece of tomato on it. However this very pretty and powerfully flavoured salad changed my mind.

2 large beetroot, boiled (not pickled), peeled and mashed
2 tablespoons *labneh* (see page 000)
275 ml/½ pint yogurt

4 to 5 cloves of garlic, crushed
salt
a few mint leaves and 2 teaspoons *labneh*

Blend all the ingredients until smooth and creamy. (Use the food processor.) Decorate with a few whole mint leaves and little dots of the extra *labneh*.

Salata turlu-turlu

Mixed salad
Turkey

This ratatouille-like salad marries most unusually with its dressing.

450 g/1 lb aubergines, sliced
1 medium onion, finely sliced
100 ml/4 fl oz, olive oil
2 green peppers, seeded and sliced
salt and freshly ground black pepper

450 g/1 lb tomatoes, peeled and sliced
300 ml/½ pint yogurt
1 clove of garlic, crushed with ½ teaspoon salt

Sprinkle the aubergine slices with salt. Leave them to drain in a colander for 30 minutes. Rinse and squeeze gently. Pat dry.

Fry the onion in the oil until soft and translucent. Add the aubergine slices and green peppers. Season and cook for 10 minutes. Add the tomatoes and simmer for 30 minutes, when the liquid in the pan should be much reduced. Chill.

Beat the yogurt with the garlic. Pour over the chilled aubergine mixture and serve.

Sweet peppers

An English friend with whom I was discussing this book said she was looking forward to lots of pepper recipes and at least one pepper salad. Alas, I am obliged to disappoint her.

Peppers play a much smaller part in Middle Eastern cookery than they do in that of Italy or Southern France, Spain or North Africa. Cooked, they are employed most by the Turks; in salads, they make some appearances, rather on the sidelines. They are of course stuffed whole (see page 87), but, otherwise, they are always cut out into little strips. (In Cyprus, no use is made of yellow and red varieties; only the green ones.)

As for a salad consisting predominately of peppers, I have to admit that I cannot find one anywhere. In fact the only pepper 'solo' I can discover is a Lebanese pickle.

Kabis flayfileh helweh

Pickled peppers
Lebanon

These peppers can be used in vegetable dishes and salads.

1 kg/2¼ lb sweet peppers	425 ml/15 fl oz white wine
2 tablespoons salt	vinegar
425 ml/15 fl oz water	1 hot chilli

Wash the peppers thoroughly. Remove their stems. Scrape out the seeds and pith. Dissolve the salt in the water, and strain the water. Add the vinegar and the hot chilli. Pierce small holes in the pepper skins and put them in a glass jar. Cover with the liquid and seal tightly. Keep for at least 3 weeks.

Note: Some people use all vinegar (without water), but I don't recommend this.

MEAT AND CHICKEN

I N THE MIDDLE EAST, meat is undoubtedly the food of first choice. To eat meat is festive and luxurious. Abstaining from it is either undertaken for religious reasons (many Greeks and Cypriots still practise the Lenten fast, and find it a genuine hardship) or enforced by poverty. Vegetarians are still regarded with bewilderment. (A friend of mine's request for a pitta containing salad but no kebab was greeted with general laughter at the Limassol Wine Festival.)

Lamb or mutton has always been the meat chiefly eaten. Kid is still available (we have cooked it ourselves in Limassol, in a stew) but is becoming much rarer. In Christian areas, pork is popular; it is much cheaper than lamb. Beef is expensive and fashionable.

The anthropologist, Lévi-Strauss, has claimed that the high status attached to roast meat is a universal characteristic. Certainly roasting, on a spit or in the oven, is the method of cooking far preferred throughout the region.

In the Hellenic world, a whole roast lamb marks the traditional celebration of the greatest feast, Easter. (Often, in the week preceding Easter, I have seen a child seated on a Limassol doorstep, cuddling a dear little lamb, and have thought of the line, '*Regardless of their fate, the little victims play.*') As well as celebrating a festival, killing and roasting a lamb has traditionally, all over the Middle East, been the greatest compliment one can pay a guest.

That great authority on cookery (most especially fish cookery), Alan Davidson has, in his delightful book of culinary essays, *A Kipper with My Tea*, produced a gripping account of a roast-lamb feast. An essay entitled 'Attacking a Lamb with our Fingers' describes the event, held in the garden of a villa near Konya in Turkey:

'Our host had had three lambs slain and roasted whole in a sealed pit oven, out of doors. We shared the general sense of pleasurable anticipation as he bade his gardener break the seal on top of the oven. Gather round, he told us, the smell will be marvellous. It was indeed appetising. But as the gardener lifted out the scorched corpses, doubts attacked us.

'The lambs had been small, and they looked smaller still after being sheared, cleaned, trussed and hung for hours in the fierce heat. A pathetic sight, in severe contast to the large, live, hungry human beings who crowded round with exclamations of joy, those of them who were yoked to photographic apparatus jostling and clicking.

'We sat at round picnic tables, eight to a table, eight to a lamb. At our table, someone (predictably, the familiar anecdote was bound to come to life) plucked out the eyes, announcing that they were the choicest morsel. Our unease was increased. But we set to work with our fingers, as directed, plucking morsels of meat. This was not the neat, easy operation which might have been expected. The flesh was still so hot that it was difficult to handle the gobbets. On the surface, it had been cooled by contact with the air; but a finger poked in to prise a piece off would be slightly burned. . . .

'What was left of the lamb's head had been decorated by placing sprigs of flat-leafed parsley between its jaws. What happened after the eyeball incident was that another lady of the party reached forward, parted the jaws and plucked out the tongue. She did this with finesse, her own uncooked tongue peeping out between her uncharred teeth as she concentrated on the task. Another great, although diminutive delicacy, it seemed. I regularly have a slice of ox-tongue for lunch at home, but I declined my share of this morsel.

'Not far away was a fountain, with towels laid out beside it. Naturally, we all wanted to wash our hands when we had finished feasting on the lamb. Naturally? Or was there something more to the want?'

As far as I am concerned, the answer must be 'Yes!'. In fact, I feel I would need a full ritual bath after such a gastronomic nightmare. In Cyprus, sucking pig is a great delicacy: again . . . not for me.

Let it be noted, however, that nowadays, in the Middle East, whole animals are cooked only comparatively rarely. Dismembered, they are roasted in many ways which are perfectly acceptable to the more squeamish carnivore.

ROAST AND GRILLED MEAT

Arni psito

Roast lamb
Greece and Cyprus

This is the classic Sunday roast that in former days used to be taken to the baker's to be cooked in his oven. (I know of one Limassol baker who still provides this service, but nowadays most people have ovens of their own.)

1 leg of lamb, weighing about 2 kg/4½ lb
3 cloves of garlic, peeled and sliced
salt and freshly ground black pepper
half a lemon
2 tablespoons olive oil

1 kg/2¼ lb medium potatoes, peeled and halved
50 ml/2 fl oz red wine mixed with 100 ml/4 fl oz water
1 teaspoon oregano (optional)
2 sprigs of rosemary
1 bayleaf

Make slits in the skin of the lamb and insert slivers of garlic. Season with salt and pepper and rub with the lemon. Brown and seal in a very hot, preheated oven (220°C, 475°F, gas 7) with the olive oil. (This will take about 10 minutes.) Now surround the meat with the halved potatoes. Pour over the wine and water mixture, with the oregano, if used. Top with the rosemary and bayleaf, and cook in a hot oven (200°C, 400°F, gas 6), basting occasionally, for about 1½ to 2 hours. The potatoes and lamb should now be brown and the liquid pretty well absorbed.

Notes: Some people don't like these soft Greek potatoes. If you want very crisp potatoes, parboil them and cook them separately.

If you are using lamb which has been frozen, it's a good idea, after de-freezing, to marinate it overnight in 4 tablespoons red wine mixed with 2 tablespoons olive oil. Turn once, and baste.

—— *Arni kleftiko* also known as *Arni Palikari* ——

Lamb 'bandit-style'
Greece (and Cyprus)

Kleftis means a thief in Greek. But the other name of this dish, *Palikari*, refers to the mountain brigands who harried the Turks in the struggle for Greek Independence. This name is a more romantic one, but in Cyprus the only term used is *kleftiko*.

The brigands wrapped the lamb in paper to prevent its smell being carried to the enemy and then buried it in an earthenware pot over burning charcoal. In Cyprus today, the earthenware pot is cooked still often cooked in the sealed, whitewashed clay ovens that look like beehives.

However, thanks to the invention of silver foil, it is perfectly possible to make *Kleftiko* in a gas or an electric oven. The result is more suitable for an informal meal than a grand dinner party, but the chunks of meat will be very tender and will have a most delicious flavour.

I give large quantities, partly because the meat shrinks during cooking, but chiefly because hungry, healthy people (this includes me, aged 80) will eat a lot of it. (It is not meant for those with tendencies to anorexia!)

2 kg/4 lb stewing lamb (try to get young fresh lamb, and not the frozen stuff), cut into chunks, each piece with a bone in it (a 7-cm/3-inch-square piece is definitely on the small side)	salt freshly ground black pepper cinnamon *rigani* (oregano) bayleaves a lemon, halved

Put all the meat in a large bowl, sprinkling lavishly with salt, pepper, ground cinnamon and – less lavishly – oregano, and turning the pieces. Rub each piece of meat with cut lemon.

On a sheet of silver foil, place two small chunks (7 × 7 cm/3 × 3 in) or one larger chunk of the lamb, with a bayleaf on top. Fold into a parcel, and put this parcel inside a second one, for there must be no leakage. Put all the parcels in a large oven-proof container. Seal this, too, with foil. Place in a preheated oven (220°C/425°F/gas 7) and cook for 2½ hours. Serve with rice or mashed potato or just bread, and wedges of lemon to squeeze over the meat.

Arnaki me filo

Lamb in filo pastry
Greece

Like the previous one, this is a 'parcel' recipe but a much more elegant one; the wrapping, as well as its contents, is delicious.

6 lamb steaks, cut from the leg, and trimmed of fat	a pinch of oregano
	freshly ground black pepper
marinade:	salt
4 tablespoons red wine	
2 tablespoons olive oil	12 sheets filo pastry
1 clove of garlic, crushed	melted butter

Marinate the steaks for at least 2 hours, or overnight, in the marinade. Drain.

Follow the general instructions for filo under *Spanakopitta* (see page 106). Brush a sheet of the filo with melted butter and top with another. Fold in half. Place a steak on the filo, and fold into a neat packet, tucking the ends under. Place the filo parcels on a buttered baking tray and brush the tops and sides with melted butter. Bake in a preheated oven (200°C/400°F/gas 6) for 20 minutes. Serve at once.

Notes: Some people wrap the steaks in blanched vine leaves (see page 90) before wrapping them in the filo. This is very attractive to look at, and adds moisture, even though the marinating should prevent the meat being dry. Other people top the steaks with a little onion, softened in butter and a slice of peeled tomato, and some add a slice of Feta or a little grated Kefalotiri, but of these alternatives I only really recommend the vine leaves.

Shish kebabi

Kebabs
Turkey

I have two provisos when it comes to kebabs (probably the form of Middle Eastern cookery most popular in Britain). It is not worth making them unless you can grill them over charcoal. They are essentially out-of-door, or at least terrace, cookery. Secondly, the marinade is an essential factor. There are those who hold that a squeeze of lemon juice and a sprinkling of salt, pepper and *rigani* are all that is necessary. If the meat is perfect, the weather marvellous, the rustic environment idyllic, this may suffice. However, Greek, Turkish, Armenian and Lebanese cooks, using different mixtures, all stress the vital importance of the marinade.

Lamb is undoubtedly the preferred meat. I agree with this view, but other meats can make good kebabs: pork, veal and also chicken can be delicious.

Let us describe the entire – very simple – process before listing some possible marinades.

1 kg/2¼ lb leg of lamb (or veal or pork)

Trim the meat, and slice it. Cut the slices into 2.5-cm/1-inch squares. Stir them in a bowl containing the marinade of your choice and leave, covered, in the refrigerator for at least 6 hours, or overnight. Thread the prepared pieces of meat onto skewers. Some people alternate them with bits of onion, bay leaves, pieces of green pepper, mushrooms, and even halved tomatoes. (I think the bay leaves make a great contribution, and sometimes use onion and pepper slices.) Cook over charcoal, turning the skewers occasionally, and basting with the marinade, for about 15 minutes. Pork will need a few minutes more. Serve on a bed of rice, with salads, or in warmed pitta bread (not grilled).

Marinades

These are very simple to prepare. However I must first say a few words about 'onion juice'. In my first book, *The Adventurous Fish*

Cook, I described a method of extracting 2 tablespoons of juice
from a large Spanish onion, as follows: 'Slice the onion finely in
rings. Lay the rings on the sloping sides of a deep plate. Lightly dust
with fine sugar and leave in a warm place for 1 hour. At the end of
that time, you should be able to collect 2 tablespoons of juice from
the well of the plate.' Absolutely true! But nowadays I use a cheap
metal lemon-squeezer (the kind with a lid that presses down on half
a lemon or orange). Substitute a peeled onion for a lemon; the juice
will pour through. (I have two of these squeezers; if you only have
one, wash it thoroughly before using it again for lemons.)
  Quantities given for marinades are for 1 kg/2¼ lbs meat.

A Greek marinade
150 ml/¼ pint olive oil
the juice of 1 lemon
the juice of 2 medium onions
2 bay leaves
2 teaspoons *rigani* (oregano)
2 tomatoes, peeled and
  chopped
salt and freshly ground black
  pepper

A Cypriot marinade
300 ml/½ pint dry red wine
2 onions, chopped
2 bay leaves
a good pinch of *rigani*
  (oregano)

A Turkish marinade
150 ml/¼ pint olive oil
the juice of 2 onions
1 teaspoon cinnamon
salt and freshly ground black
  pepper

A Lebanese marinade
75 ml/3 fl oz olive oil
the juice of 1 onion
100 ml/4 fl oz dry red wine or
  vinegar
½ teaspoon allspice
salt and freshly ground black
  pepper

A yogurt marinade can also be used. For this 300 ml/½ pint yogurt
is mixed with the juice of an onion and salt and black pepper.
Personally, I think a yogurt marinade is more successful with
chicken than with meat. Although I give other chicken recipes at the
end of this chapter, I feel that the following one belongs here with
the other kebabs.

Chicken kebabs

Use chicken breasts, skinned and boned and cut into 2.5 cm/1 inch cubes.

6 chicken breasts

Yogurt marinade:
300 ml/½ pint yogurt
2 cloves of garlic, crushed

salt and freshly ground black
  pepper
1 teaspoon ground cumin
the juice of a lemon

A marinade of oil and lemon juice is also good for chicken kebabs:

100 ml/4 fl oz olive oil
100 ml/4 fl oz lemon juice
1 clove of garlic, chopped
1 teaspoon paprika

½ teaspoon dried mint
salt and freshly ground black
  pepper

This marinade was given to me by a Lebanese friend: you may want to halve the quantity of lemon juice.

Sheftalia

Little sausages
Cyprus

Although my other recipes for minced meat follow later, sheftalia definitely belong here. They are an integral part of Cyprus kebab-making.

When you order a kebab in Cyprus, you ask for 'plain' if you just want the cubed lamb or pork (known as *souvlakia*). If you want these little sausages as well, you ask for 'mixed'. Or your kebab can consist of *sheftalia* alone: if this is your requirement, ask for them by name or as 'the sausages'.

Sheftalia are easy to make, and I think more people should make their own sausages in Britain, where 'bangers' are often far too bready. (I hear that 'research has proved' to the giant manufacturers that most people don't want their sausages to taste of anything at all. However, if this were your view, I doubt if you would be reading this book.)

Making sausages for grilling is easy, as the skins don't have to be 'sewn up' to prevent the filling escaping into the frying pan. People flinch from the idea of the skins, but these are so 'aesthetic' that, when you buy them from the butcher, they should cause you no unease. In Cyprus, you can also buy them from grocers: these ones look just like cling-film, while the butcher's look like cling-film with a delicate marbling of fat. Jane Grigson describes them as the 'frilly' mesentery of the pig. Ask your butcher for 'skins for sausages'. In Cyprus they are called *panna*.

To make 14 little sausages:
1 onion, finely chopped or grated
450 g/1 lb mince (some people use pork, some half pork and half lamb; others specify half coarsely and half finely ground mince. I don't think any of this really matters. However, the mince should not be too lean)
3 tablespoons parsley, finely chopped
1 heaped tablespoon fine breadcrumbs
1 egg (optional)
1 teaspoon salt
½ teaspoon freshly ground black pepper
½ teaspoon powdered cinnamon (optional but good)
100 g/4 oz *panna* (see above)

Mix all the ingredients together with your hands or in the food processor. Dip the *panna* in warm water (some people soak it in cold water and vinegar for a few minutes, but I don't) and unroll it. Cut it into rectangles about 7 × 12 cm (3 × 7 inches). Take a dessert-spoonful of the mixture and roll this into a small sturdy sausage. Put it on its piece of *panna* and fold in the edges to form a nice little parcel.

These sausages should be grilled over charcoal. They are ideal for barbecues. However you *can* cook them under an ordinary very hot grill. Cook until very brown, turning once. Serve with salad and pitta bread.

STEWS

These are an omnipresent feature of Middle Eastern cookery. When you think of cooking, without hotplates or gas rings, over charcoal or in clay ovens or, more recently, on paraffin stoves, you will understand one traditional reason for the one-pot recipe. Stews, also, however, promote that glorious melding of herbs and spices with olive oil, onions, garlic and tomatoes which is so characteristic of Middle Eastern food.

I have a theory (perhaps it is just a dream, but I don't think so) that, in culinary terms, the 'Affected Eighties', with their 'artistic' dishes so often composed with an eye to colour rather than flavour, are going to yield to the 'Natural Nineties', and to good food, attractively garnished but not obsessively 'tarted up'. I am encouraged by hearing that one of London's most expensive restaurants is now making a feature of *boeuf bourguignonne*, a perhaps smarter but close relation of the recipe that follows.

Stifado

Stew with onions
Greece

This classic Greek stew is nowadays often served in an emasculated form, with little cubes of meat, insufficient onions and sometimes no garlic, and an inferior (not olive) oil. This is a tragedy. Ideally, from my point of view, *stifado* should be made with hare. Rabbit will do – and so will beef.

750 g/1½ lb small pickling onions, peeled
150 ml/¼ pint olive oil
1 kg/2¼ lb jointed hare or rabbit *or* beef, cut into pieces rather than cubes
175 ml/6 fl oz red wine
100 ml/4 fl oz red wine vinegar

1 tablespoon tomato paste and 2 ripe medium tomatoes, peeled and chopped
3 to 4 cloves of garlic, crushed
2 bay leaves
1 cinnamon stick
salt
freshly ground black pepper
a pinch of cumin (optional)

Brown the onions in the olive oil, and then set them aside. Now brown the meat. Add all the other ingredients (except the onions) and simmer slowly for 1½ hours. Add the onions, and cook very slowly for another hour. Allow to stand for 10 minutes before serving with crusty bread.

Notes: The small onions should remain whole; you may want to add them even later.

If you have a crock pot (slow cooker), it is excellent for this dish.

Fassolakia me kreas

Green beans with meat
Greece and Cyprus

I find the Greek way of making simple stews like this one, with a dominant vegetable but always onion and tomato in the background, very sympathetic.

Early every morning, my wife, going swimming, sees the proprietor of a small glass-walled café she passes starting off a *yahni* (stew) of one kind or another. You can make it with pork or chicken instead of lamb, and your dominant vegetable can be cauliflower, aubergines, spinach, okra, peas – whatever looks best in the market or shop. My particular favourite is the combination of lamb with French beans.

1 kg/2¼ lb French beans
100 ml/4 fl oz olive oil
1 large onion, peeled and cut into slices, vertically
1 kg/2¼ lb good stewing lamb, cut into pieces but not boned

500 g/18 oz ripe tomatoes, peeled and chopped
1 litre/1¾ pints water
½ teaspoon cinnamon
salt and freshly ground black pepper

Top and tail the beans and cut them in half, but no smaller. Trim the sides with an apple corer (there must be no strings). Wash and drain.

Make the oil very hot in a heavy saucepan; soften the onion in it, and then add the pieces of meat, browning them rapidly. Add the beans and shake the pan, or fork through it, for a minute or two.

Add the tomatoes and cook rapidly for another 5 minutes, stirring or forking occasionally. Now add the water, cinnamon and seasonings. Bring to a vigorous boil, and stir. Lower the heat and simmer, partly covered, for about 1½ hours.

Serve with rice, potatoes or good bread.

Tas kebabi

Braised lamb
Turkey

I'm pleased to see my friends, the green peppers, playing a (comparatively) large part here.

1 kg/2¼ lbs lamb, boned and cubed
50 g/2 oz unsalted butter
2 medium onions, finely chopped
3 large green peppers, seeded and chopped
3 large tomatoes, peeled and chopped

150 ml/¼ pint water
½ teaspoon allspice
salt and freshly ground black pepper
2 tablespoons parsley, finely chopped

In a heavy pan, brown the meat in half the butter. Remove the meat and add the rest of the butter. Cook the onions and peppers in it until softened. Add tomato, spices, seasoning and water, and 1 tablespoon parsley. Return the lamb to the pan and simmer until tender (for about 1½ hours) on low heat. Sprinkle with the remaining parsley before serving.

Serve with *Hunkar Beyendi* (see page 98) or with rice.

Tavas

Lamb casserole with cumin
Cyprus

The *tava*, after which this dish is named, is a casserole of unglazed terracotta, with a closely fitting lid. In the old days, when most people did not own ovens, the *tava* would be buried in the ground on a bed of fiery charcoal embers (see *kleftiko* page 127) to cook slowly to perfect tenderness.

This is Cypriot cooking at its simple best, and very characteristic in its reliance on *artisia* (cumin). If your casserole lid does not fit really tightly, seal it with foil. *Tavas* should not need added fat or liquid, but I add a small quantity of water to be on the safe side.

1 kg/2¼ lb leg or shoulder of lamb, boned and cut into pieces ('cubed', if you like)	2 teaspoons ground cumin salt
2 large onions, sliced	freshly ground black pepper
450 g/1 lb ripe tomatoes, peeled and sliced	100 ml/4 fl oz water

Place the lamb with the onions and tomatoes in an unglazed casserole. Stir in the cumin and seasonings, and add the water. Seal tightly, and cook at 150°C/300°F/gas 2 for up to 3 hours. Check after 1½ hours and add a little more water, if necessary. (It ought not to be.)

This dish is always served with *pourgouri pilafi* (see page 76). Some people sprinkle on more cumin at the table.

Arni fricassé

Fricassee of lamb
Greece

This spring-time recipe satisfies two of my passions: for *avgolemono* sauce and for cooked lettuce (far preferred by me to the insipid raw salad ingredient).

1 kg/2¼ lb lamb, cut into 'serving-size' pieces	1 tablespoon parsley, chopped
50 g/2 oz unsalted butter	1 teaspoon mint, chopped
1 bunch spring onions, peeled and chopped (including the green stems	1 tablespoon dill (or fennel), chopped
4 heads Cos lettuce, quartered and scalded with boiling water	salt and freshly ground black pepper
	avgolemono sauce (see page 158)

Sauter the meat in the butter. Add the onions and cook for a few minutes more. Just cover with water and add seasonings and herbs. Simmer until the meat is tender (for about 1½ hours). Add the lettuce and cook for a further 15 minutes. Drain off the liquid from the pan, and keep the pan-contents warm in a serving-dish, while using the strained liquid to make an *avgolemono* sauce. Pour the sauce over the meat and lettuce. Serve with rice, potatoes or crusty bread.

Note: Other vegetables can be used instead of lettuce: the fronded chicory (called endive by some), artichoke hearts, very young broad beans still in the pod (the Greek mangetout), or small whole (topped and tailed) courgettes.

Afelia

Pork stew
Cyprus

I have described the *Afelia* cooking method – unique to Cyprus – in relation to vegetables (see page 108). However, if you see the word *Afelia* by itself on a Cypriot menu, or if you ask for *Afelia* in a restaurant, it will be made, as follows, with pork.

500 g/18 oz lean pork from fillet, loin, leg or shoulder, boned and cut into cubes
300 ml/½ pint red wine
freshly ground black pepper
½ teaspoon salt

1 tablespoon coriander seeds, crushed
½ teaspoon cumin (optional)
a stick of cinnamon
1 bayleaf
3 tablespoons olive oil

Leave the pork cubes overnight in a marinade of all the other ingredients except the oil. Turn at least once.

Drain the pork, reserving the marinade. Remove the bayleaf and cinnamon stick. Make the oil very hot. Cook the pork in it, fast, until browned all over, and just cooked through. Add the marinade to the pan, cooking for about 30 minutes until the liquid has much reduced. This is often served with *pourgouri pilafi* (see page 76).

Hirino me kithonia

Pork with quinces
Greece

This recipe is unusual, since the Greeks do not normally use fruit –
apart, of course, from lemons – in their cookery. I wonder what
Greek discovered the harmony between pig and quince? (Cooking
apples can be substituted for quinces in this recipe, but I find the
result inferior.)

1 kg/2¼ lb pork, cut into
   'serving-size' pieces
50 g/2 oz unsalted butter
300 ml/½ pint red wine
150 ml/¼ pint water
a piece of lemon peel
a pinch of cinnamon
salt and freshly ground black
   pepper

1 kg/2¼ lb quinces, peeled,
   cored and thickly sliced
2 tablespoons brown sugar

garnish:
1 tablespoon parsley, finely
   chopped

Brown the pieces of pork in the butter. Add the other ingredients,
except the quinces and sugar, and simmer for 1 hour.

Meanwhile, sprinkle the sliced quinces with the sugar. Put them
on top of the meat and pour any liquid drawn from the quinces on
top. Cook very slowly for about 1 hour more, rocking the pan
occasionally – rather than stirring – to avoid breaking up the fruit.
Serve garnished with parsley.

Budugov miss

Lamb chops with apricots
Armenia

Irresistibly my thoughts move from pork with quinces to lamb with
apricots: a romantic combination. This recipe has the added
advantage (provided you remember to soak the apricots) of being
unusually quick and easy to prepare.

6 lamb chops
35 g/1½ oz unsalted butter
1 small onion, chopped
    (optional)
½ teaspoon cinnamon
a pinch of cumin

a pinch of coriander
50 g/2 oz sultanas
175 g/6 oz dried apricots,
    soaked overnight in cold
    water and drained

Brown the chops and the onion, if used, in the butter in a heavy pan. Add the remaining ingredients and just cover with water (about 300 ml/½ pint). Bring to the boil. Then simmer gently, stirring occasionally, for 30 minutes. (If the chops are not quite tender, you may need a little longer.) Serve with rice.

Khoresht-e-albaloo

Meat stewed with cherries
Iran

I have moved right out of my territory. The Iranian *khoresht* is a mixture of meat, spices and, often, fruit. Here, sour cherries make an exciting and unusual dish which I can't resist including. Morello cherries are probably the best variety to use in Europe. If you can only get hold of sweet cherries, adjust the flavour, which should be tart, with extra lemon juice. I cannot advise using tinned cherries. Use lamb or beef for this dish, but the meat must be lean, so trim off any fat.

1 kg/2¼ lb lean stewing lamb
    or beef, cubed
75 g/3 oz unsalted butter
1 large onion, finely sliced
1 level teaspoon powdered
    cinnamon
1 level teaspoon turmeric

300 ml/½ pint water
salt and freshly ground black
    pepper
2 tablespoons lemon juice
450 g/1 lb stoned sour black
    cherries
2 tablespoons sugar

Brown the cubes of meat in the melted butter in a heavy pan. Then, with a slotted spoon, set them aside, and cook the onion until soft. Add in the cinnamon and turmeric, and cook, stirring constantly, for 2 minutes. Return the meat to the pan and add water, salt, pepper and the lemon juice. Cover and simmer for 45 minutes. Add the stoned cherries and sugar, and simmer for 10 minutes.

Now taste the sauce. It should be more sour than sweet, but it should not be bitter. If too sweet, add more lemon juice. If unpleasantly sour, you could add more sugar. If you make either of these additions, cook for a further minute or two to allow the extra ingredients to merge.

Serve with *chelau* rice (see page 64).

Variation: It is possible to replace the cherries with an equal quantity of sour grapes. I haven't tried this because the idea makes my tongue curl up.

MINCED MEAT

Mince has always played an important part in Middle Eastern cookery. This has been both for reasons of economy and from the need to make the best of meat not always of the highest quality. The kneading and pounding – predecessors of modern mincing – of chopped meat could always (eventually!) reduce it to a condition in which it would be both tender and palatable.

Minced meat dishes have already appeared in other sections of this book (see, for instance, *kibbeh*, pages 71–74 and stuffed vegetables, pages 85–92). In the recipes that follow, minced meat is the dominant ingredient.

——————— *Moussaka* ———————

Greece

(We all know what this is, but I find it impossible to translate. Instead, let me note that the emphasis goes on the *third* syllable, not the second.)

Moussaka is made in Cyprus as well as Greece, but never satisfactorily from my point of view, as potato always seems to be included. Also – this happens in Greece, too – a *béchamel* sauce is used instead of a kind of custard I regard as the right topping. Some people will disagree with me about these matters, but here is *my* traditional moussaka.

450 g/1 lb aubergines
salt
100 ml/4 fl oz olive oil
2 medium onions, finely chopped
450 g/1 lb lean lamb, minced very finely (I put it through the food processor)
2 large ripe tomatoes, peeled and chopped
1 tablespoon parsley, finely chopped
salt and freshly ground black pepper

for the 'custard':
300 ml/½ pint milk
the yolks of 2 large eggs
salt and freshly ground black pepper
a pinch of cinnamon

Slice the aubergines, salt them, and leave them in a colander to drain for 30 minutes. Then squeeze gently to extract moisture. Rinse thoroughly in cold water, and dry with a cloth or kitchen paper.

Heat the olive oil and fry the aubergine slices, turning once, until golden. Set the aubergines aside, using a slotted spoon. Now soften the onions in the oil, add the mince, and brown. Add the tomatoes, parsley and salt and pepper to taste.

Oil a deep baking-dish. Put in alternate layers of aubergines and the meat mixture, starting and finishing with aubergines.

Now beat together the milk and egg yolks with the salt, pepper and cinnamon. Pour this into the baking dish, and bake for approximately 45 minutes at 180°C/350°F/gas 4. The moussaka should now have a bubbly golden-brown crust.

This is wonderful hot, and also very good cold.

Kafta bil-saniya

Meat loaf
Lebanon

Here are two distinctively Middle Eastern meat loaves, one to be eaten hot and the other cold. Both are easy to make if you have a food processor. (The mince must be reduced almost to a paste; you would have to spend a lot of time with pestle and mortar.)

1. *bi-tahina*

with tahini

675 g/1½ lbs lean lamb or
   beef, very finely minced
2 medium onions, minced
2 tablespoons parsley, finely
   chopped
salt and freshly ground black
   pepper

for the sauce:
3 tablespoons tomato paste
3 tablespoons wine vinegar
½ teaspoon allspice
2 tablespoons tahini
a pinch of cayenne
water

garnish:
2 teaspoons parsley, chopped

Mix the loaf ingredients thoroughly together (preferably in a food processor). Put the mixture in a buttered loaf tin and bake at 230°C/450°F/gas 8 for about 15 minutes until lightly browned. Meanwhile prepare the sauce, mixing all the ingredients together, and then thinning them with water to the consistency of a thin cream. Pour half of this over the meat loaf in the tin. Bake at 200°C/ 400°F/gas 6 for 1 hour.

Turn onto a serving dish and garnish with parsley. Heat the remaining sauce and serve as an accompaniment.

2. *bi-joz wa fustu' halabi wa snaubar*

with nuts

750 g/1½ lbs lean beef,
   minced to a paste
1 teaspoon allspice
½ teaspoon paprika
1 teaspoon salt
2 cloves of garlic, crushed
1 tablespoon walnuts, ground
   fine
1 tablespoon pistachio nuts,
   ground fine

2 tablespoons pine nuts
1 beaten egg (optional)

for cooking:
225 ml/8 fl oz wine vinegar
   mixed with
100 ml/4 fl oz water

garnish:
1 tablespoon parsley, finely
   chopped

Mix all the loaf ingredients thoroughly together, preferably in a food processor. Lightly oil the bottom of a large cooking pot. In the pot, shape into a rounded oval loaf. I add the egg when mixing the ingredients, to make this easier, but it is not in the original Lebanese recipe. Cover the loaf with the vinegar and water mixture and cook very, very slowly for 40 minutes. Drain off the liquid and chill the loaf thoroughly. Garnish with parsley.

James.

Izmir koftesi

Smyrna sausages
Turkey

Natalie : Sept 2nd 1993.

The Greek version of this dish is called _soudzoukakia_. I would prefer to give it on political grounds as the Turks were responsible for a hideous massacre of Greeks at Smyrna. However, culinary considerations must come first, and the Greek version omits the green peppers which greatly enhance the sauce.

2 slices of white bread, crusts removed
675 g/1½ lb finely minced lean ~~meat~~ Lamb.
3 cloves of garlic, crushed
1 egg, beaten
1 large onion, grated
1 tablespoon parsley, finely chopped
1 teaspoon ground cumin
salt   & Coriander freshly ground.
freshly ground black pepper
flour for coating
olive oil for frying
1 tbsp Chopped Green Chillis.

for the sauce:
750 g/1½ lb ripe tomatoes, peeled and chopped (2 cans Chopped toms).
2 large green peppers, seeded and minced
2 teaspoon sugar
2 bay leaves
salt and freshly ground black pepper
~~100 ml/4 fl oz water~~ white (Pne).
1 tbsp. Balsamic Vinegar.

Soak the bread in a little cold water for a few minutes. Squeeze out the moisture. Mix the mince, garlic, bread, egg, onion and the parsley and cumin together thoroughly. Season with salt and pepper. Roll the mixture into fat little sausages and coat them with flour.

Mix all the sauce ingredients, and simmer them over low heat until soft, reduced and entirely melded.

Fry the sausages in hot olive oil until lightly browned. Put them in an oven dish. Pour the sauce over them and put in a moderate oven, 180°C/350°F/gas 4, for 10 minutes. Serve with rice.

Kanellonia

Pancakes with a meat filling
Cyprus

As far as I know, these substitute *canneloni* are Cypriot. Certainly, served as the first course of Sunday lunch, they are a pleasing alternative to the dreaded *pasticcio* of both Greece and Cyprus: this baked slab of macaroni, glued together with an insufficiently cheesy sauce and dotted with bits of mince, like currants in a suet pudding, is my pet aversion. People keep telling me that they have eaten good *pasticcio*, but it has never come my way.

for the batter:
100 g/4 oz plain flour
1 to 2 eggs (some people use up to 4, which makes for very heavy pancakes)
300 ml/½ pint milk
½ teaspoon salt
25 to 50 g/1 to 2 oz butter, for frying pancakes

for the filling:
50 g/2 oz butter
1 medium onion, finely chopped
450 g/1 lb finely minced meat

1 tablespoon parsley, finely chopped
½ teaspoon powdered cinnamon
salt and freshly ground black pepper
1 tablespoon flour
100 ml/4 fl oz milk

garnish:
1 to 2 tomatoes, peeled and chopped
50 g/2 oz Kefalotiri or Parmesan cheese, finely grated

Mix the batter and leave it to stand for 30 minutes.

In a heavy pan, melt half the butter and soften the onion in it. Add the minced meat, parsley, cinnamon and seasoning, and cook for about 20 minutes. If it seems too dry, add a little water, to prevent the mixture sticking.

Meanwhile make a roux with the remaining butter and the flour. Add the milk and stir till thickened. Blend this sauce with the meat mixture.

Now make the pancakes, frying them in as little butter as possible, and stacking them on a plate as you go.

Put 1 heaped tablespoon of filling on each pancake and roll it up. Line up the pancakes in a buttered square oven dish. Sprinkle the tomato decoratively over the top, together with the grated cheese. Brown in the oven or under a grill and serve at once.

Keftedes

Meat rissoles
Greece and Cyprus

These crisp and savoury meatballs can be the size of a small egg, suitable for a main dish, or of walnut-size, to serve with drinks or as part of a mezé.

To make 3 dozen walnut-size keftedes:

500 g/18 oz fine mince of good quality (you can use lamb, beef or pork)	1 tablespoon fine breadcrumbs
	¼ teaspoon cinnamon
	¼ teaspoon dried mint, powdered
1 medium onion, peeled and grated	1 tablespoon olive oil
225 g/8 oz raw potatoes, grated very finely (after which you can squeeze the moisture out of them with your hands)	1 teaspoon salt
	½ teaspoon freshly ground black pepper
	3 tablespoons parsley, finely chopped
1 egg, beaten	olive oil for frying

Mix all the ingredients thoroughly together. I put them in the food processor. Roll into balls. (Our friend, Androula Costi, does 2 at a time, rolling 1 in each hand.)

Heat the oil until it sputters. Then fry the balls rapidly until dark brown. Drain on kitchen paper and transfer to a serving dish. At their best hot, I think, but also good when cold.

KIDNEYS, BRAINS, LIVER

The Americans describe these as 'variety meats'. To me, they have always been known as offal, and with no pejorative overtones. Apparently, today's less robust Britons shun this term as well as the animal parts concerned.

Like the French, Middle Eastern cooks make good use of every part of an animal. The results are often splendid. However I can sympathise with those who do not want to make a traditional *Patsia* or *Mayeritsa* (see pages 30, 31) or to get involved with tongues, let alone eyes (see page 125).

But when it comes to kidneys, brains, liver . . . I find revulsion, on the part of anyone who cooks and eats meat at all, hard to comprehend. These foods are so easy to prepare – and the resulting dishes so rewarding.

I hope the following five recipes will encourage you at least to try.

Kilawi bi-asir al-rumman

Kidneys with pomegranate juice
Lebanon

I am very fond of lamb (as opposed to pig or ox) kidneys, and for years have cooked them in a wine sauce. Since living in Cyprus I have discovered two delicious new ways of cooking them, both from the Lebanon.

8 lamb kidneys, trimmed, skinned and cut in half lengthwise
75 g/3 oz unsalted butter
2 cloves of garlic, crushed
salt and freshly ground black pepper
a good pinch of paprika, of cayenne and of cinnamon
75 ml/3 fl oz pomegranate juice (see page 184)
1 tablespoon parsley, finely chopped

Sauter the kidneys with the garlic in the melted butter. Add the salt and spices, stirring, and then the pomegranate juice. Simmer for about 5 minutes very slowly. Serve with rice.

Kilawi ma' al-hamud

Kidneys in lemon sauce
Lebanon

8 lamb kidneys, skinned and trimmed	25 g/1 oz flour
50 g/2 oz unsalted butter	3 tablespoons lemon juice
1 onion, thinly sliced	salt and freshly ground black pepper

Sauter the whole kidneys lightly in the butter. Remove them to a plate and slice them thinly, seasoning them with salt and pepper. Cook the onion in the pan until golden brown. Add the flour and cook for 1½ minutes, stirring. Pour in the lemon juice and, still stirring, cook for another 2 minutes. Return the kidneys to the pan, mixing with the onions. Cook for a final 2 to 3 minutes. This rather homely dish is delicious with mashed potatoes.

Miala tiganita

Fried brains
Cyprus

Perhaps this recipe is the best possible introduction to brains – very easy to cook and so crisp and delicious.

6 sets lamb brains	unsalted butter for frying
water	flour for coating, seasoned with salt and pepper
1 tablespoon salt	
1 tablespoon vinegar	

I usually buy frozen lamb brains from New Zealand, each neatly bagged in plastic inside the cardboard packet. Whether you use fresh or frozen brains, you must soak them for 1 to 2 hours in cold water to cover, with a little vinegar and salt. Rinse thoroughly, then remove the thin outer membrane (this isn't at all alarming) and rinse again. Now put the brains in a pan of salted water at simmering point. Cook but do not boil for 15 minutes. Drain, dry with paper towels and cut into slices. Dip the slices in seasoned flour, and fry gently in butter until golden brown. Serve at once, with wedges of lemon.

Note: This sauce is absolutely untraditional, but I often have fried brains with 25 g/1 oz unsalted butter heated until turning brown. At this point I add the juice of half a lemon and 1 tablespoon of chopped capers.

―――――――――― *Miala me lemoni* ――――――――――

Brains with lemon
Cyprus

Quite different, and even easier to cook, this recipe is designed to be eaten as a salad. The texture is delicious, rather like that of poached mushrooms.

6 sets lamb brains
3 tablespoons virgin olive oil
1 tablespoon lemon juice
salt
freshly ground black pepper

2 tablespoons parsley, finely
   chopped
½ teaspoon powdered cumin
4 spring onions, finely chopped

Prepare the brains as for *miala tiganita* (see page 147) but this time bring them to the boil in salted water. Reduce the heat and simmer for 20 minutes. Drain and cut into slices and mix, while still warm, with a dressing made from all the other ingredients. Allow to cool, then chill.

―――――――――― *Soda bil-khall* ――――――――――

Liver with vinegar
Lebanon

The frequent use of vinegar in Arab cookery originated in the Muslim prohibition of wine. I prefer the forbidden alternative in most cases, but here (red wine) vinegar contributes to the spicy vigour of the dish.

65 g/2½ oz unsalted butter
1 medium onion, finely chopped
3 to 5 cloves of garlic, crushed with salt and mixed with ½ teaspoon dried mint
500 g/18 oz lamb's or calf's liver, sliced

2 tablespoons flour
a good pinch each of cinnamon, paprika and cayenne pepper
2 teaspoons salt
150 ml/¼ pint red wine vinegar

Melt the butter in a heavy frying pan, and cook the onion at medium heat until it starts to brown. Stir in the crushed garlic. Now add the sliced liver, and cook, turning, for about 10 minutes. Stir in the flour, spices and salt and pour in the vinegar. Bring up to the boil, then reduce and simmer for 10–15 minutes.

Serve with rice or mashed potatoes.

CHICKEN

Chicken can become the most boring of foods in various circum-stances: if you always cook it in the same way; if you buy frozen chicken; if you buy factory-raised ('broiler') chicken.

My wife once cooked 'broiler' chicken in London, in a lemon sauce. Someone said to her, 'That fish was delicious.' The taste of fishmeal on which these unfortunate birds are fed pollutes their flavour intolerably.

Freezing – perfectly acceptable for many foods – has a terrible effect on chicken meat, in my view. It makes it tough and insipid. In Cyprus, I have never bought a frozen chicken. I buy fresh *horiatiki* (village) chickens. They are delicious and the stock from them jellifies after 1 hour in the fridge or at room temperature in cold weather. My advice is: spend a little more on fresh – ideally, free-range – chicken, and this food will again become the treat it used to be. Also, since chicken is never very expensive, compared to meat, experiment with it. Here are some suggestions.

Mouloukhia ala dajaj

Chicken '*Mouloukhia*'
Egypt

Mouloukhia is a variety of mallow from which the Egyptians make a soup which is a major part of the diet of the poor. When they have no meat or chicken stock, they cook it with water. The leaves have a unique taste. I like to use them as part of a main dish, the way they are usually eaten by the better off. One can use meat for this dish, but I am not fond of boiled meat, I prefer chicken, as cooked by our Arabist friend, Meric Dobson, formerly of Beirut and now of Nicosia.

1 chicken
2 to 2½ litres/3 to 4 pints water
salt
1 onion and 1 carrot (optional)
4 rounds of Arab bread
225 g/8 oz dried *mouloukhia* leaves *or* 2 kg/4½ lb fresh *mouloukhia*, the stalks removed and the leaves finely chopped

2 large onions, finely chopped and soaked in lemon juice or wine vinegar
2 tablespoons oil *or* 40 g/1½ oz unsalted butter
6 cloves of garlic, crushed with a little salt
1 tablespoon ground coriander seed
a good pinch of cayenne
225 g/8 oz rice

Cook the chicken until tender in the salted water. You could add a carrot and an onion to enrich the stock. Meanwhile, split the Arab bread into halves and then into quarters and bake it in the oven till crisp and brown. Prepare the chopped onion mixture.

When the chicken is cooked, take it from the stock, bone it, and chop the meat into bite-size pieces. Keep these moist in a little of the stock. (If you put vegetables with the chicken, remove them now.)

Bring the stock to the boil. Crumble the dried *mouloukhia* into it, and boil for about 20 minutes. (Fresh *mouloukhia* is very difficult to obtain in England – it is in Cyprus, too! – but you will find packets of the dried leaves in Greek and Oriental provision stores. If you do find fresh *mouloukhia*, cook it for half the time.)

Towards the end of the *mouloukhia's* cooking time, fry the crushed garlic in the oil or butter. Add the coriander and cayenne and fry a little longer till it forms a thin paste. Add to the soup and cook for another 2 minutes, stirring gently.

Most people crumble the Arab bread in the bottom of their soup plates. I prefer to scatter it on top. The pieces of chicken, reheated in the stock they have been standing in, will then be put in, and the soup poured over them, as a lavish sauce.

This dish is served with rice. (If you have plenty of stock, you could use some when you cook the rice according to the method on page 65). It is also accompanied by the chopped onion mixture.

Kotopoulo me avgolemono
Chicken with egg and lemon sauce
Greece

1 large chicken
1 onion, chopped
salt and freshly ground black
   pepper
1 bayleaf
Avgolemono sauce (see page
   158)

garnish:
2 teaspoons parsley, finely
   chopped (optional)

Cut the chicken into joints and large pieces. Cover with water and poach gently with onion, salt and pepper and bayleaf. Do not overcook; the chicken should be tender, but not falling apart. Keep the cooked chicken pieces warm in a little of the stock. I sometimes remove any coarse skin from the chicken at this stage. Make an *avgolemono* sauce, using strained stock from the chicken. Pour over the chicken and serve.

Despite my love of parsley, I sometimes don't even garnish this dish because it is so pure and delicate (guaranteed to tempt an invalid or fussy convalescent, by the way). Some people add a handful of rice to cook for the last 20 minutes with the chicken, but I find this messy. Serve rice cooked separately (if you have more stock than you need for your sauce, cook the rice in this).

Çerkes tavuğu

Circassian chicken
Turkey

Georgia also claims this dish, which was probably introduced into Turkey by the beautiful Circassian slaves whom the Turks captured in the Caucasus.

1 large chicken (1.5 kg/3 lb)
1 onion, chopped
1 carrot, chopped
salt and freshly ground black pepper
3 slices white bread, crusts removed
175 g/6 oz walnuts
½ teaspoon paprika

2 cloves of garlic, crushed
 (optional, though not to me)

garnish:
1 tablespoon walnut oil
½ teaspoon paprika
1 tablespoon parsley, finely chopped (optional)

Cut up the chicken, and poach it gently with the onion, carrot and salt and pepper until tender. This will take around 1 hour. Remove the chicken from the stock and allow to cool a little. Now remove the flesh from the bones, cutting it into strips about 5 cm/2 inches long and 1.2 cm/½ inch thick. Return the chicken skin and bones to the stock, and cook until reduced by half. Strain the stock. Use a little to keep the chicken pieces moist.

Grind the walnuts, paprika, garlic and bread in a food processor. Add the strained stock gradually till you have a thick, smooth sauce.

Mix half the sauce with the chicken strips, and shape into a mound on a serving dish. Coat with the rest of the sauce. Mix the walnut oil and paprika thoroughly and, just before serving, dribble this over the chicken. If you like, garnish with parsley, but I like the plain red and cream effect.

Note: As with all Middle Eastern recipes, there are differences of viewpoint. Some like this dish warm. I like to prepare it in advance for a summer lunch party. Some people omit the garlic, but I think this makes the dish excessively bland.

Chicken Soraya

I begged this recipe from Soraya Antonius, an authority on Arab cookery and a marvellous cook (see *Fattoush*, page 110). The pickled lemons are a Moroccan speciality. This is somewhat off my beat, but since a Middle Eastern cook served this in the Middle Eastern city of Nicosia, I feel justified in including it.

Soraya Antonius is hostile to giving quantities of spices, olive oil and seasonings. She feels that these should be left to the taste of the cook.

olive oil	freshly ground black pepper
1 large onion, chopped	cumin
1 large chicken	375 ml/½ pint chicken stock,
3 or 4 pickled lemons*	approximately

Cook the onion until soft in the oil. Add the chicken, cut into pieces, and brown thoroughly. Now add 3 or 4 pickled lemons, cut into quarters vertically. Add stock to about a third of the way up the ingredients, and season with black pepper and cumin. Simmer until only a little thick juice remains of the liquid.

* *Pickled lemons*

450 g/1 lb ripe firm lemons	coarse salt (*gros sel*)
a bayleaf or two	water

Divide the lemons down vertically into 4, leaving them sufficiently joined at the top to hold together, while you pack them with coarse salt. Put them in a preserving jar with a bay leaf or two. Fill up with water, making sure that the uppermost lemon is quite covered. (You could put a stone or piece of wood on top.) Leave for 1 month in a dark place. Should keep for several months.

—————— *Dajaj bil-bahar al-helou* ——————

Paprika chicken
Lebanon

This is the Lebanese version of what is usually classified as a
Hungarian dish.

1.5 kg/3¼ lb chicken,
    quartered
3 tablespoons olive oil
2 tablespoons wine vinegar
1½ teaspoons paprika
salt and freshly ground black
    pepper to taste

3 cloves of garlic, crushed

garnish:
1 tablespoon parsley, finely
    chopped

Sauter the chicken in the olive oil and put the pieces in an oven-
proof dish. Thoroughly mix all the other ingredients with the oil
remaining in the pan, and pour over the chicken. Bake at 180°C/
350°F/gas 4 for about 45 minutes. Garnish with parsley.

    Serve with rice or mashed potatoes.

—————— *Purdah Pilau* ——————

Chicken Pilaf
Iraq

Alas, I was never offered this 'Arabian Nights' delicacy in Kirkuk or
Baghdad, where its origins lie, but the version cooked by Meric
Dobson makes it quite impossible for me not to include it here. It
is spectacular.

1 chicken
salted water to cover
50 to 75 g/2 to 3 oz clarified
    butter
1 medium onion, finely
    chopped
2 to 3 cloves or garlic, chopped
    small
3 or 4 whole cloves
3 or 4 whole cardamons
1 stick of cinnamon, about 1
    cm/½ inch long
a large pinch of allspice

1 cup (225 g/8 oz) rice
¼ teaspoon saffron soaked in 2
    or 3 tablespoons water and
    drained *or* a large pinch of
    turmeric (not as good)
50 g/2 oz sultanas, soaked in a
    little water
25 g/1 oz blanched almonds
    or pine nuts
1 packet (370 g/13 oz) 'Jus-
    rol' puff pastry
1 or 2 sliced eggs (optional),
    hardboiled

Cook the chicken and cut it up as for *Mouloukhia* (see page 150).

Melt the butter. In it fry the onion and garlic with the spices (not the saffron) until soft. Add the washed rice and fry until translucent. If using saffron add it now, and then add 300 ml/½ pint of the liquor in which you have cooked the chicken. Salt to taste. Cover the saucepan, and simmer till the rice is cooked and all the liquid absorbed. Meanwhile fry the soaked sultanas with the nuts until golden. Mix them into the rice, when it is cooked.

Roll out the pastry thinly into a circular shape. Butter a 1-litre/2-pint soufflé dish or equivalent ovenware dish. Line it with the pastry, which will hang over the edge.

Fill the pastry case with the alternate layers of chicken and rice. A few people add hardboiled eggs. Now fold the edges of the pastry inwards, and press together to seal. Dot with small pieces of butter and bake at 190 to 200°C/375 to 400°F/gas 6 for 40–45 minutes until brown.

Turn out onto a serving dish. It is a great moment when you cut the 'veil' . . . and reveal the luscious *houri* within!

Serve with yogurt or with *Talatouri* (see page 120).

Mousakhan

'Chicken in envelopes'
Lebanon

Chicken is 'veiled' again here, but much more simply than in the preceding recipe.

2 small chickens, quartered	salt and freshly ground black
225 ml/8 fl oz olive oil	pepper
2 large onions, thinly sliced	1 teaspoon sumac (see page
4 rounds of Arab bread	186)

Bring the chicken quarters to the boil in salted water and simmer for 20 minutes. Drain them, and brown them in half the olive oil, and then remove them to a side dish. Lightly brown the onions in the same oil you used for the chicken.

Halve the rounds of Arab bread, and rub the insides of them with the rest of the olive oil. Now season the chicken pieces with the salt, black pepper and sumac. Put a quarter chicken inside each half round of bread and divide the fried onion among them. Cook in a baking tin at 180°C/350°F/gas 5 for 40 minutes. (If the bread shows signs of burning, put some foil over it.) Serve only salad with this dish.

SAUCES AND DRESSINGS

I T IS OF neccessity that this is the shortest section of my book.
There are very few Middle Eastern sauces in our sense of the
word.

The reason is not far to seek; a glance through this book will
provide it. Oil or butter, lemon, tomato, onion, garlic, herbs and
spices are part of the actual cooking process. Dishes such as stews
(see pages 133–140) create their own delicious 'built-in' sauces.
Even 'dry' dishes do not need added flavour. Kebabs, for instance,
have been marinated in savoury mixtures (see page 129). Greek
roast lamb (see page 126), rubbed with lemon and, studded with
slivers of garlic, aromatic rosemary and bay leaf, does not need to be
helped down with mint sauce or redcurrant jelly.

Of the few sauces that follow, it seems to me that only one rivals
the really great sauces of the European tradition. This is the
avgolemono, Byzantine in origin and, in delicacy of texture and
flavour, a champagne among sauces. It also has the advantage of a
marvellous adaptability.

There are those who, in my view, pollute this sauce by adding
flour, or even cornflour to it. This not only weighs it down but robs
it of its uniqueness.

Salsa avgolemono

Egg and lemon sauce
Greece

2 egg yolks
the juice of a good-sized lemon
1 tablespoon cold water

300 ml/½ pint stock (chicken,
   meat, fish or vegetable)
salt

Using a whisk, beat the egg yolks in a bowl with the lemon juice until frothy. Add the cold water, beating it in.

Allow your stock, heated to boiling point, to stand and cool for 3 minutes. Pour a spoonful of stock into the egg and lemon, whisking the while, then another spoonful, then a third. Now, very gradually, add the rest of the stock, beating all the time until it thickens. Season with salt to taste.

This sauce *can* be reheated, but it must never be allowed to boil. It can also be served cold. In either case you can add chopped herbs – parsley, dill or fennel, for example – just before serving.

Note: You may notice that in my recipe for *avgolemono* soup (see page 32), I use whole eggs instead of just the yolks. For the large quantity of liquid in a soup this is quite all right, but just the yolks are better for a sauce.

Tahiniyeh

Tahini sauce
all over the Middle East, especially in Arab countries

You will find little saucers of this on your table in most Middle Eastern restaurants in London, and in every restaurant in Cyprus, for you to dip your bread into. Its principal ingredient is the sesame-seed paste, tahini (see page 186).

2 to 3 cloves of garlic, crushed
   with a little salt
the juice of 2 medium lemons

150 ml/¼ pint tahini
salt

Stir the garlic with a little of the lemon juice. Add the tahini, mixing thoroughly. Then beat in (by hand or in the food processor) the rest of the lemon juice, adding a little cold water till you have achieved the consistency of double (not whipped) cream. Season to taste with salt.

Variations: Some people– especially the Lebanese – like this sauce to be very lemony, and use as much lemon juice as tahini.

If you don't like garlic, omit it; Cypriots sometimes do.

You can include 1 tablespoon of finely chopped parsley in the mixture.

In Cyprus, many people enrich *tahinosalata*, as they call it, by beating in 4 tablespoons of olive oil.

Other possible additions are half a teaspoon of powdered cumin, or of cayenne pepper, if you like a hot sauce.

You can garnish with a sprinkling of pepper.

This sauce is often eaten with fish. I have heard that it is also sometimes used as a salad dressing.

Tomato sauce

Tomato sauces are often served with pilafs, with roast or grilled meat and – nowadays – with pasta. I give you 2 recipes, one very straightforward, the other highly spiced.

Domata salsa

Tomato sauce
Greece

50 g/2 oz butter *or* 4
  tablespoons olive oil
2 tablespoons onion, grated
1 kg/2¼ lb ripe tomatoes,
  peeled and chopped
1 teaspoon sugar
1 teaspoon *rigani* (oregano),
  dried and crushed

1 tablespoon parsley, finely
  chopped
salt and freshly ground black
  pepper
1 bayleaf

In the heated butter or oil, cook the onion for a minute or two. Then add the rest of the ingredients. Simmer until you have a thick purée. You could add a little water, if the sauce seems too thick.

Note: I, of course, would add 2 cloves of crushed garlic to the grated onion. I might also include a glass of dry red wine.

If you use oil instead of butter, you could keep this sauce in a glass jar for several weeks. Cover the top with a thin layer of olive oil and close tightly.

Dukkous al-tamata

Tomato sauce with spices
Gulf States

I can't resist including this sauce, though it is not from 'my' Middle East. In the original version of this sauce, *baharat* (a traditional mixture of spices) is used. I have made my own approximation to it.

2 tablespoons olive oil	½ teaspoon paprika
4 to 8 cloves of garlic, crushed	¼ teaspoon ground coriander
1 kg/2¼ lb tomatoes, peeled and coarsely chopped	¼ teaspoon ground nutmeg
	¼ teaspoon ground cloves
2 to 4 teaspoons salt, to taste	¼ teaspoon ground cinnamon
½ teaspoon freshly ground black pepper	a good pinch of cumin

Heat the oil in a pan. Add the garlic and stir round for about 1 minute. Add the tomatoes and salt and simmer, covered, for 20–30 minutes. Add the spices, stirring in well, and cook, uncovered, for another 3 minutes.

This is often served with pilafs and also with roast meat.

Skordalia

Garlic sauce
Greece

This is strictly for those who love garlic. There are other recipes in this book where you could reduce the garlic, or even omit it. But not this one!

8 slices day-old white bread, with crusts removed	150 ml/¼ pint olive oil
6 to 8 cloves of garlic, peeled	3 tablespoons white wine vinegar *or* 2 tablespoons
salt	lemon juice

Soak the bread in a little water for a few minutes. Meanwhile, pound the garlic, with a little salt. (This is one of those few recipes where my friend the food processor just won't do.) Now squeeze the water out of the bread with your hands, kneading it until soft and smooth. Next, pound it with the garlic until they are amalgamated. Gradually add the olive oil, first drop by drop, then in a thin stream, continuing to pound all the time until the oil is absorbed. Finally, stir in the wine vinegar or lemon juice.

Some people also stir in 1 tablespoon of chopped parsley; others enrich the sauce with the yolk of an egg.

This sauce is usually eaten with fried fish. It is good with grilled fish, too, and with fried aubergines or courgettes.

Tarator

Garlic sauce with nuts
Turkey

This has a strong resemblance to *Skordalia,* but with the interesting addition of walnuts. In Egypt and Lebanon, they use pine nuts instead, so I have indicated this as an alternative.

3 thick slices day-old white bread, with crusts removed	3 to 6 cloves of garlic, crushed
100 g/4 oz ground walnuts (or pine nuts)	6 tablespoons olive oil
	1 teaspoon salt
	3 tablespoons lemon juice

Soak and squeeze the bread as for *Skordalia*. You can use a food processor to blend it with all the other ingredients to a smooth thick creamy paste.

This, like other sauces I refer to, is usually eaten with fish. (I think the reason for this preponderance of fish sauces is that fish cannot be cooked at length with oil, tomato, garlic, herbs and spices, as tougher foods can.) It is also eaten with grilled chicken and sometimes with boiled vegetables.

When eaten with fish, the sauce is sometimes thinned with fish stock to a pouring consistency.

Yogurt sauce

Many dishes in this book are eaten accompanied by a bowl of yogurt: a perfect natural sauce, healthy and delicious.

Here is a variation for moderate garlic lovers.

Yogurt salsasi
Yogurt sauce
Turkey

1 to 2 cloves garlic, crushed
  with ½ teaspoon salt
300 ml/½ pint yogurt

garnish:
½ teaspoon dried mint
  (optional)

Mix the garlic and salt thoroughly with the yogurt. Serve in a bowl, with the dried mint crumbled over the top, if you like.

Latholemono
Oil and lemon sauce
Greece and Cyprus

You will find this sauce (sometimes without the chopped parsley) on the table of every café in Cyprus, in Worcestershire-sauce bottles, so that you can shake it vigorously before sprinkling it over your food. (This is the sauce I refer to in connection with *Trout Maryland*, page 50.) What a splendid alternative to Britain's tomato ketchup!

275 g/½ pint extra-virgin olive oil	1 tablespoon parsley, very finely chopped
2 tablespoons lemon juice	salt and freshly ground black pepper

Beat the olive oil and lemon juice together. Add the parsley and salt and pepper. You must serve this at once – or in a shakeable container, as the olive oil and lemon juice will separate if left to stand.

Please use virgin olive oil, if you can, for this and the dressings that follow. (See also Oil, page 183.)

Use to accompany fish, or sprinkle on cooked vegetables.

Salad dressings

Salad dressings in the Middle East, as in all other civilized cuisines, are made of good olive oil and either lemon juice or wine vinegar.

The proportions are, in general, 3 parts olive oil to 1 part lemon juice or wine vinegar. In some places, such as Lebanon, the national passion for lemon juice may result in a larger proportion of it being used. (I have heard of equal parts of olive oil and lemon juice.) But let us set out the classical instructions, in manageable quantities:

3 tablespoons (preferably extra-virgin) olive oil	salt and freshly ground black pepper
1 tablespoon lemon juice or wine vinegar	

To this, many people, including me, often add 1 to 2 cloves of crushed garlic.

Other additions are parsley, mint, *rigani* (oregano), dill, fresh coriander, and in each case, the herb should be finely chopped.

THE SWEET COURSE

I BROODED ON THOSE words 'the sweet course', for a long time
before I wrote them down. This was not because I was wondering
whether to refer to 'sweets', 'desserts' or even 'puddings' (as some
fossilized members of society still inaccurately call everything from
an apple pie to a water ice). It was because, in the Middle East, 'the
sweet course' doesn't exist.

Most British people, asked about Middle Eastern sweets, conjure
up pastries filled with raisins, nuts and spices and soaked in honey
or syrup. In Greek, Lebanese, Turkish or Iranian restaurants in
London, at the end of a meal, you can ask for *baklava* or *katayfi* (the
ones like shredded wheat) and the proprietors, familiar with British
eccentricities, often accede to such requests. However, no one from
this part of the world would dream of eating such a treat in such
circumstances.

'Treat' is the right word, for these sticky delights are loved by
Middle Eastern people. But pastries and other sweet confections
are enjoyed in the middle of the morning, in the afternoon, or when
visitors call in the evening. They are never eaten at the end of lunch
or dinner.

I am not – alas – a baker or confectioner. I never make cakes, and
hardly ever make pastry (see page 106). I am only . . . a cook. If you
feel the desire for a syrup-soaked pastry, my advice is that you – like
people in the Middle East – should go to a cake shop to satisfy it.
Please don't think me rude; I am just being honest.

This does not mean that I am going to desert you after your main course. After all, I am English, and myself often enjoy something sweet at the end of a meal. I have found that the Middle East can offer solutions to the problem of 'the sweet course' that are far more appropriate (and healthy) than layers of filo impregnated with syrup. These fall into three categories: sweets involving fruit (both fresh and dried), sweets made from rice or semolina, and what I shall call 'instant' sweets.

FRUIT

Fresh fruit is of course what you will always be offered at the end of your meal. Summer lunches in Cyprus invariably end with chilled sweet melon, green or golden, and water melon with its beautiful colour contrast between rosy flesh and black seeds, its crisp texture and pure, wonderfully refreshing flavour. (Melon is always eaten at the end of the meal, never, British-style, at the beginning.)

Cyprus is still a seasonal country in terms of what produce you can buy, and we follow the course of the year in its fruits. First come the loquats (sometimes delicious, sometimes tasteless; the crop varies in an inexplicable way from year to year). Then there are strawberries, cherries, plums, apricots and peaches; next come melons and grapes. Pomegranates are followed by the winter staples: apples and pears from the mountains, oranges and mandarins and, in recent years, locally grown bananas.

Fruit becomes ever more popular in Britain, and the fruit bowl is regularly filled in most homes. However, we all hunger for variety, and people here are no exception to this rule. I give some suggestions for ways of varying fresh fruit.

Compôtes

The Turks will frequently offer you a *kompostu* at the end of a meal, and the Greeks, somewhat less frequently, will offer you a *komposto*. This, of course, is our old friend, the compôte: fruit in a syrup. Sometimes the fruit is cooked, and sometimes not. I recommend that you try accompanying these compôtes with yogurt instead of cream.

Rothakina komposta

Peach compôte
Greece

This Greek recipe is particularly simple and delicious, and, of course, here, as in almost all the fruit recipes that follow, you can reduce the (usually high) sugar content to suit your taste.

1 kg/2¼ lb fresh peaches
3 tablespoons lemon juice
175 g/6 oz caster sugar

Dip the peaches first in boiling water and then in cold, for easy peeling. Cut them in half, stone them and then slice them. Sprinkle the slices first with lemon juice and then with caster sugar. Refrigerate them for at least an hour. If you have fresh mint, a sprig or two looks pretty as a garnish.

Ayva kompostu

Quince compôte
Turkey

1 kg/2¼ lb quinces, peeled,   3 cloves
    cored and quartered   2 tablespoons lemon juice
900 ml/1½ pints water   450 g/1 lb caster sugar
1 piece cinnamon bark

Place the quinces in a saucepan with the water, cinnamon, cloves and lemon juice. Simmer until nearly tender. Stir in the sugar and cook for another 10 minutes, when the liquid will be a deep clear amber. Allow to cool, and then chill.

Portokalia syropata

Oranges in syrup
Greece

I like this recipe because the orange peel in the syrup gives a touch of tartness.

4 fresh seedless oranges
2 tablespoons orange flower
    water (optional)

175 g/6 oz caster sugar
425 ml/¾ pint water

Mark the peel of the oranges into quarters with a sharp knife. Put them in a bowl and cover with boiling water. Leave for 5 minutes. Then drain and peel; the pith will come away with the skins. Reserve the skins. Slice the oranges across, thinly, and put in a bowl. Pour over the orange flower water, if used.

Put the sugar and water in a saucepan. Grate peel from the skins of at least 2 of the oranges into the water. (Take care not to grate the inner pith.) Bring to the boil, and cook the syrup at moderate heat, stirring till it thickens enough to coat the spoon. Leave to cool, then pour over the sliced oranges, and chill.

Apithia se krassi

Pears in wine
Greece

425 ml/¾ pint dry red wine
175 g/6 oz caster sugar
2 pieces cinnamon bark
3 cloves

the peel of a lemon
6 firm whole pears, peeled,
    with stems left on

Heat the wine in a saucepan big enough to hold the pears. Stir in the sugar, cinnamon, cloves and lemon peel and simmer for a minute or two. Lay the pears in the pan, and cook them very slowly until they are tender but not soft. Transfer the pears to a bowl. Reduce the syrup, at high heat, by about half and strain it over the pears.

This looks very pretty . . . not quite as pretty is the similar recipe I have used in an emergency:

1 (approx) 550 g/19 oz tin of
    pear halves in syrup
275 ml/½ pint dry red wine

2 teaspoons powdered
    cinnamon
50 g/2 oz dates, chopped

Keep 150 ml/¼ pint of the syrup from the tin. Put it with the pears, wine and cinnamon in a pan. Bring to the boil, then lower heat and simmer, covered for 10 minutes. Remove from the heat. Add the chopped dates, and leave to cool.

Fresh fruit sorbets

The Turks make the most delicious fresh-fruit water-ices, which are very easy to prepare.

———————— Çilekli dondurma ————————

Strawberry water ice
Turkey

600 ml/1 pint water
225 g/8 oz caster sugar
2 teaspoons lemon juice

450 g/1 lb strawberry purée
    (675 g/1½ lb whole
    strawberries, mashed and
    sieved)
4 tablespoons milk

Stir the water and sugar in a heavy pan until the sugar is dissolved. Add the lemon juice and bring to the boil. Leave to cool, then combine with the strawberry purée and milk. Freeze in a freezer tray or box.

You can make *Kiraz dondurma* (cherry water-ice) by the same method, substituting the same quantity of cherry purée (made by liquidizing stoned cherries in the food processor) for the strawberries.

Limoni serbeti

Lemon sorbet
Greece

Here is an alternative method of making a water-ice.

1 tablespoon powdered gelatine	1 tablespoon grated lemon peel
1.2 litres/2 pints water	175 ml/6 fl oz fresh lemon juice
450 g/1 lb caster sugar	

Soften the gelatine in 4 tablespoons of the water. Boil up the rest of the water with the sugar. When the sugar has melted, remove from heat, stir in the gelatine until dissolved. Now mix in the lemon rind and juice. When cool, put into freezer trays or box, stirring occasionally with a fork. It should take about 4 hours to freeze.

For orange water-ice, substitute double the quantity of fresh orange juice for the lemon juice, but use the lemon rind, and add 2 tablespoons lemon juice.

Stafylia zaharomena

Frosted grapes
Greece

This isn't really a fresh-fruit recipe ... more a little fantasy for the frivolous. The grapes should be white, seedless, not too small, and in perfect condition.

450 g/1 lb grapes	175 g/8 oz icing sugar
1 egg white	

Divide the grapes into small bunches. Rinse, drain and dry with a cloth or kitchen paper. Now beat the egg white until frothy but not stiff. With a pastry brush, coat each grape with egg white. (It doesn't take all that long!) Place a wire cake-rack on a tray, and put the little bunches of grapes on the rack. Sieve icing sugar over them until they are well coated. Put the tray in the refrigerator until the sugar has set.

Dried fruit

Far more use is made of dried fruit in the Middle East than in Britain. All the sweets that follow are very characteristic of Middle Eastern style.

—————————— *Khoshaf* ——————————

Dried fruit salad
Lebanon

This exotic concoction crops up all over the Middle East, but this version is from Lebanon. For *khoshaf*, the fruit is macerated, not cooked in the syrup.

450 g/1 lb dried apricots, of
   very high quality
225 g/8 oz seedless raisins
225 g/8 oz caster sugar
1.2 litres/2 pints water
1 teaspoon rose water

1 teaspoon orange flower water
225 g/8 oz blanched and
   skinned almonds *or* almonds,
   pine nuts, walnuts and
   skinned pistachios

Dissolve the sugar in the water. Add the fruit and flavourings and leave overnight. Mix in the nuts, and chill.

Note: You may need more rose and orange flower water. Varieties of these essences vary greatly in strength; some are strong distillations; others are much weaker and cheaper. I would use 1 tablespoon of each of the very inexpensive Cyprus varieties are available in every grocer's shop here.

—————————— *Hosaf* ——————————

Dried fruit salad
Turkey

Most of the ingredients of this are similar to those of *Khoshaf*. But *Hosaf* lacks the rose and orange flower essences and it is cooked.

225 g/8 oz sugar
1.2 litres/2 pints water
100 g/4 oz dried apricots
100 g/4 oz prunes, pitted
100 g/4 oz seedless raisins

100 g/4 oz dried figs
225 g/8 oz mixed nuts:
blanched and peeled almonds
with walnuts, skinned
pistachio and pine nuts

Dissolve the sugar in the water. Boil for 5 minutes. Add the dried fruit and cook for another 20 minutes, stirring. Now stir in the nuts and cook for another 5 minutes. Cool and then chill.

Absolutely untraditional note: I have been known to stir in a large tot of rum before chilling. I would not do this with *Khoshaf*, because of the delicate flavour of the essences.

Izmir kompostu

Smyrna fig compôte
Turkey

Figs have always been a speciality of Smyrna. You used to be able to buy them in wooden boxes for Christmas . . . perhaps you still can but I doubt it.

450 g/1 lb dried figs
600 ml/1 pint water
blanched almonds
175 g/6 oz sugar
a piece of lemon rind

the juice of a lemon
3 tablespoons honey (optional)

garnish:
chopped blanched almonds or
chopped walnuts

Soak the figs in water for only about 1 hour, till they're just soft enough to handle. Drain and insert a blanched almond through the base of each.

Now, in a pan, dissolve the sugar in the (heated) water. Add the lemon rind, juice, and honey, if used. Bring to the boil. Add the figs to the syrup, bring back to the boil, and then cook very gently until the figs have plumped out, and are tender. Transfer them to a bowl. Pour the syrup over them. Cool, then chill. Garnish with the chopped nuts.

Note: I use the optional honey in this recipe, for its flavour, but I omit 50 g/2 oz of the sugar.

Hrisomila peltes

Apricot cream
Greece

The original material for a dish very similar to this used to be made in various parts of the Middle East, including Cyprus. It is called *armar ad-din* by the Arabs, and you will still find the sheets of dried apricots in some Middle Eastern provision shops. A Cypriot friend of mine tells me that her grandmother was the last person whom she knew had made it in Cyprus, 50 years ago, but small quantities are still imported. The sheets are soaked for several hours, then boiled and simmered till they turn into a thick purée.

Amar ad-din is very expensive and not always easy to find. I make a modern Greek version, using dried apricots:

450 g/1 lb dried apricots	75 g/3 oz almonds, blanched
sugar to taste	and cut into slivers
	whipped cream

Use very good dried apricots for this. Completely cover them – but no more – with water, and soak them overnight. Transfer them, with the water they have been soaking in, to a pan, and simmeer them until soft. Now sieve the apricots and liquid or put them in a food processor to purée. Return to the saucepan, and add sugar *to taste* (I don't like it too sweet). Add the almonds, and heat, stirring constantly, till the sugar has melted. Cool and then chill.

Note: Forget about the yogurt, this time. Clotted or whipped cream always accompanies this.

Rice and semolina

Perhaps you are overcome by unsatisfactory childhood memories? Forget them. These 'rice puddings' taste different.

It is very interesting to find how they crop up under different names, and with small variations, all over the Middle East. Because of the comparative shortage of dishes for 'the sweet course', this is particularly noticeable.

Rizogalo

Rice with milk
Greece and Cyprus

2 tablespoons short-grain rice	1 small piece lemon peel
100 ml/4 fl oz water	1 pellet mastic, crushed
575 ml/1 pint milk	(optional: see below)
3 tablespoons sugar	1 tablespoon rose water

Wash the rice and soak it in the water for 30 minutes. Bring the milk, with the sugar and lemon peel added, to the boil. Then add the rice and water. Cook very slowly until almost all the liquid has been absorbed. (Add the mastic now, if you are using it.) Remove from the fire, cool for a moment, and then add the egg yolk, beaten with a tablespoon of cold milk. Stir in the rosewater, and cool, then chill.

Notes: mastic is a kind of resin which Greeks and Cypriots use as chewing gum. I personally don't like it in rice pudding. If you don't use it, sprinkle a little cinnamon on top of the rice before serving.

The Arabs make a very similar version of rice pudding, *Roc bi-halib*, but they use more sugar and add orange flower water instead of rose water.

Muhallabiyeh

Rice cream
It's everywhere!

This is the most popular 'rice pudding' throughout the region. It seems to be eaten everywhere except in Greece. *Muhallabiyeh* is the Arabic name. In Cyprus, this has become *mahallepi*. The recipe I give is a Lebanese one.

1.2 litres/2 pints milk
60 g/2½ oz ground rice
100 g/4 oz sugar
2 teaspoons orange flower
    water
½ teaspoon rose water

garnish:
chopped walnuts,
blanched chopped almonds,
peeled pistachios

Make a paste of the ground rice and some water. Bring the milk to the boil and add the ground-rice paste. Stir over low heat until the mixture thickens: about 20 minutes. Don't allow it to stick. Add the sugar, and go on stirring until the mixture coats your wooden spoon. Add the orange flower and rose water. Serve cold, sprinkled with the chopped nuts.

Note: Just the almonds will do for garnish.

Moghli

Ground rice with aniseed
Lebanon

Traditionally served on the birth of a son, this Arab dish tastes very strange to Europeans. I include it largely for interest, but if you are fond of aniseed, and like the exotic, why not try it?

125 g/4 oz ground rice
1.5 litres/2¼ pints water
125 g/4 oz caster sugar
1 teaspoon aniseed
½ teaspoon caraway seed
a pinch of cinnamon

a pinch of ground cloves
a pinch of ground ginger

garnish:
a mixture of chopped walnuts,
    pine nuts and blanched
    almonds

Mix the ground rice and the spices to a smooth paste with a little of the water. Bring the rest of the water and the sugar to the boil. Remove from heat and gradually stir in the rice-and-spice paste. Return to the heat and bring to the boil again, then reduce heat and simmer very slowly, stirring frequently, until the liquid has thickened enough to coat the spoon. (This will take at least an hour.) Cool and chill. Garnish with the nuts, which are usually arranged in a decorative pattern.

Mamouniyeh

Semolina pudding
Lebanon

This dish is a speciality of Aleppo, and the Syrians eat it for breakfast. However, most Arabs today regard it as a sweet. It is sometimes compared to *halva*, sometimes to porridge. My English title is, in the circumstances, a drab one.

100 g/4 oz unsalted butter
100 g/4 oz semolina
½ teaspoon powdered
  cinnamon
100 g/4 oz sugar
100 ml/4 fl oz water
100 ml/4 fl oz milk

garnish:
100 g/4 oz mixed blanched
  almonds and pinenuts, tossed
  in a little butter

Melt the butter over a low flame and gradually stir in the semolina and cinnamon. Set aside. Bring the sugar, water and milk to the boil. Lower heat and stir until the sugar has melted. Bring the semolina back to the stove and, over a very low heat, gradually stir in the liquid, continuing to cook and stir until the mixture coats the spoon. This sweet is left to rest for ten minutes, and then eaten warm, garnished with the nuts tossed in butter, and with a little cinnamon and caster sugar sprinkled on top.

'Instant' sweets

These have nothing whatsoever to do with 'instant puddings' in packets. Next only to fruit, they are the most natural sweets one can imagine.

Yogurt with honey

I am sure you never buy those disgusting yogurts with fruit ready-mushed in the carton. However, I do understand one reason why some people do. There are many who feel an aversion to the very slightly sour taste of yogurt.

In Cyprus, most yogurt is made from sheep's milk (most of the goat's milk is made into cheese). I hear that nowadays in Britain, cow's, sheep's and goat's milk yogurts are available. The Greek strained kind is widely available, and is preferable to that very set, rather 'blancmange-y' kind produced by some mass manufacturers. Many of the supermarkets sell a wide variety of yogurts.

Put a helping of good yogurt in a bowl. Over it pour a large spoonful of your favourite honey (a wonderful assortment is available in Britain today). Mix the yogurt with the honey as you eat it. This is a treat of which I never tire.

Cheese with honey

Perhaps you recoil in horror from this suggestion, but wait a minute. Cream and whey cheeses are eaten as sweets in many countries. The French eat cream cheese with fresh cream poured over, the Italians beat it up with egg yolks and beaten egg whites (sometimes they add a little kirsch). In Tuscany, Ricotta is eaten with ground coffee beans mixed with caster sugar. This brings me to my point.

The Cypriot Anari, and the Greek Mizithra are cheeses similar to Ricotta: soft and unsalted. In Cyprus, when fresh Anari comes into season, the Cypriots eat it with a pinch of cinnamon and spoon of honey. I do too, and I suggest that when, at the end of a meal, you feel that compelling urge for a taste of sweetness, you try a small helping of this healthy delight. If you can't get fresh Anari or Mizithra, get Ricotta ... or make your own *Labneh* (yogurt cheese: see page 180), which is often enjoyed in the Arab world in precisely this way.

Culinary Notes

THESE NOTES ARE intended to provide a very simple guide to ingredients for the recipes in this book. If you are interested in cooking Middle Eastern food, you will need to know about all of them, and to add them – or most of them – to your store cupboard.

Some of these ingredients – though not most of them – are expensive: regard these as a culinary investment, noting that, on the whole, they are only used in small quantities.

Bread

Bread is loved – indeed, you might say revered – all over this part of the world. It accompanies every meal and is eaten in large quantities.

In Greece and Cyprus, the staple bread, *psomi*, is the torpedo-shaped or round loaf with a thick golden crust. In Cyprus, this loaf is always round; a wholemeal version is becoming increasingly popular. Apart from this 'staff of life', there are all sorts of other breads, such as *koulouri* (covered with poppy and sesame seeds), *elioti* (olive bread) and *flaounes*, the special Easter bread containing cheese, often mint, and vast quantities of eggs.

The traditional bread of the Arab world is flat; usually with a hollow 'pocket' inside. This bread is made from various types of flour and in various thicknesses, sizes and shapes. When, on page 110, Soraya Antonius specifies 'Arab bread, not *pitta*,' she requires the thin (round) Lebanese loaf, rather than the thicker (oval) one, made only to hold kebabs, which is traditional in Cyprus. The ingredients are the same; it is the texture that differs. Both these would be described as *pitta* in Britain.

Pitta – I use the term interchangeably with Arab bread – is now widely available from shops in Britain. If you can't find it, or would like to make it yourself, here is a standard recipe from Arto der Haroutunian's *Middle Eastern Cookery*.

Khubz Arabi
Arab bread (pitta)
. . . easy to prepare and the recipe below will make about 8 loaves.

15 g/½ oz fresh yeast *or* 7 g/¼   450 g/1 lb plain flour
    oz dried yeast   ½ teaspoon salt
1 teaspoon sugar
about 300 ml/½ pint tepid
    water

Place the yeast and sugar in a small bowl, dissolve in a few tablespoons of the warm water and set aside in a warm place for about 10 minutes or until it begins to froth.

Sift the flour and salt into a large bowl. Make a well in the centre and pour in the yeast mixture. Add enough of the warm water to make a firm, but not hard, dough.

Knead on a floured working top for 10–15 minutes or until the dough is soft and elastic. If you knead in a tablespoon of oil it will make a softer dough.

Wash and dry the mixing bowl and lightly oil it. Roll the dough around the bowl until its surface is greased all over – this will prevent the dough going crusty and cracking while rising. Cover the bowl with a damp cloth and set aside in a warm place for at least 2 hours until the dough has doubled in size. Transfer the dough to the working top, punch down and knead for a few minutes. Divide the mixture into 8 pieces. Roll them between your palms until they are round and smooth.

Lightly flour the working top and flatten each ball with the palm of your hand, or with a rolling pin, until it is about 0.6 cm/¼ inch thick and is as even and circular as possible. Dust the tops with flour and cover with a floured cloth. Leave to rise in a warm place for a further 20–30 minutes.

Preheat the oven to 230–240°C, 450–475°F, gas mark 8–9 putting in 2 large oiled baking sheets half-way through the heating period. When the oven is ready slide the rounds of dough on to hot baking sheets, dampening the tops of the rounds to prevent them browning, and bake for 10 minutes. Do not open the oven door during this time, but after that it is safe to open it to see if the *pitas* have puffed up. Slide on to wire racks as soon as you remove from the oven. They should be soft and white with a pouch inside.'

Butter

Butter is the only fat, as opposed to oil, I use in cooking. A liking for tinned 'shortening' current in Cyprus today ruins many a good recipe which requires butter. If you are worried about cholesterol, use less butter, or olive oil where possible.

In the Middle East, pure butter fat (*samneh* in Arabic; you may be more familiar with the Indian word, *ghee*) is the traditional cooking fat.

My view is that you should never use salted butter for cooking: always the unsalted kind (what Americans call 'sweet' butter). However, even unsalted butter contains impurities. Ideally, for all the recipes in this book that require butter, you should use *clarified butter*.

Clarified butter

Put 450 g/1 lb unsalted butter in a large frying pan. Let it melt over very low heat until it bubbles. It must not change colour. Remove it from the heat and leave it for 2 minutes. While it is still warm, pour it through a sieve lined with a piece of butter muslin or cheesecloth, wrung out in warm water. Place a storage jar under the sieve. Keep the jar of clarified butter in the refrigerator. It will keep almost indefinitely.

Cheeses

Cheeses in the Middle East are not made for eating at the end of a meal. Most of them are very salty. The meal at which cheese is chiefly eaten (with bread and perhaps a few olives) is breakfast.

Otherwise its main use is as an ingredient in cookery.

Here is a list of the most frequently encountered cheeses:

Anari

This is a Cyprus whey cheese, similar to Ricotta. When fresh, it is sometimes eaten with honey (see page 176). Dried, I find it a thin, unsatisfactory cooking cheese. I would suggest Cheddar or Edam (or a mixture of the two) as an alternative.

Feta

This crumbly white cheese is made from sheep's (or sometimes's goat's) milk in Greece and Cyprus. Similar cheeses are made in Turkey, Iran and several Balkan countries. It is used in cookery (see pages 97, 106, 128), is an essential ingredient of a *horiatiki salata* (see page 117) and often appears in a mezé (see page 26).

Haloumi

This cheese is very popular in Lebanon, Greece and Cyprus. It is traditionally made from sheep's milk, but cow's milk is also used. In Cyprus, it is flavoured with dried mint, in Lebanon with black cumin seeds. I find it rubbery, except when fried or grilled (see page 27). For cooking, it seems to me salty and rather 'thin'.

Kasseri

This Greek sheep's or goat's milk cheese is creamy-coloured, firm and rather salty. It is good fried, like Haloumi, with a squeeze of lemon juice.

Kefalotiri

The meaning of this word is 'head cheese'. This is my favourite of all Middle Eastern cheeses for cooking, though given the choice I would probably substitute the fuller-flavoured Parmesan. I sometimes nibble a slice of it.

Labneh

This cheese is very easy to make from yogurt, as follows:

600 ml/1 pint yogurt
1 to 2 teaspoons salt, to taste

Mix the salt with the yogurt. Put it in a piece of damp muslin or soft cotton cloth, either lining a sieve or colander, or hung up with the corners tied together over a bowl (the former is simpler!). Allow to drain overnight; the whey will drip away, leaving a soft white cheese, mild and pleasant. Some people eat it with a little olive oil, and salt and black pepper or paprika. You can eat it with honey (see page 176). It is also used in various recipes. (See *salata wardiyeh*, page 122.)

Mizithra
This is an unsalted Greek soft cheese, made from sheep's milk. You could substitute fresh cottage cheese. It can be eaten as a sweet (see page 176).

Garlic

If you do not like garlic, it will be very difficult for you to appreciate – or cook – Middle Eastern food. A terrible bourgeois refinement – and perhaps the prejudice of northern tourists – has led to a diminished use of the divine bulb in Greece and in Cyprus, resulting in the castration of various dishes. (They become eunuchs!) Try to learn to like garlic. I always err on the lavish side in my recommendations, and you could start with smaller quantities.

Herbs

You cannot cook Middle Eastern food successfully without a variety of herbs.

Bay leaves
Not a herb, really, but it fulfils a herbal function, adding savour to many dishes. We have two bay trees in our Cyprus garden, but they are much harder to grow in Britain. However, the leaves are easy to find in packets.

Coriander
(See page 115.) I deal with the seeds under *Spices*.

Dill
The feathery leaves give a delicate flavour of aniseed. Fennel can be used instead. Fresh dill is a strong feature of Greek winter and spring cookery.

Fennel
Very similar to dill, fennel's aniseed flavour is considered more subtle by many people.

Mint
Sometimes fresh but most especially when dried, mint is a very important herb in Middle Eastern cookery. Grow some – in a pot if you haven't got a garden – and keep dried mint always on your herb shelf.

Oregano (also *Rigani*)
This deliciously pungent herb is used, in moderation, in many of the recipes in this book. *Rigani*, the kind of oregano that grows wild in Greece and Cyprus, is *not* marjoram, as some people say. This has led to terrible culinary errors.

Parsley
See page 116. I cannot overstress the importance of this herb in Middle Eastern cooking, and very often you need the flat-leafed Mediterranean kind. If you agree with me that its flavour is superior (and if you want to follow recipes in this book where it is essential), try growing it from seed. It is widely available in Britain now.

Purslane
See page 116.

Rosemary
This is used when cooking lamb (see *Arni Psito*, page 126) by the Greeks, Turks and Cypriots, and in recipes for preserving fish (see *Psari Marinato*, page 58).

Lemons

Lemon juice is a 'constant' in Middle Eastern food. In Cyprus (quite apart from the trees, weighted with fresh lemons for most of the year, in our garden), pure lemon juice is available in 'sprinkler' glass bottles and costs practically nothing. I have seen pure lemon juice in Britain, too (rather expensive and curiously pallid). Be sure of a supply of fresh lemons. I know they are expensive, but you *need* them.

Nuts

These appear in many of the recipes in this book. They are very popular in Middle Eastern cookery, and I have made suggestions for replacing meat with them in some recipes. We are all familiar with walnuts, almonds and pistachios, but not perhaps with pine nuts (also known as pine kernels), which occur most frequently of all. These are the kernels of the umbrella pine that grows in the Mediterranean region. They are easily found in Britain nowadays, but are expensive.

Olive oil

As I never 'deep fry' foods, I have no oil but olive oil in my kitchen. (Cf *Butter*, above.) I am delighted to see the ever-growing appreciation in Britain of this magnificent gift of Nature. All other oils are inferior; none of them can in any circumstances be used in dishes that are to be eaten cold; least of all in salads, where I believe the use of the more expensive extra-virgin olive oil is often justified. Oils other than olive oil leave a nasty film on cooked foods. Olive oil amalgamates with other ingredients, though a dish cooked with it should always be left to stand for a few minutes to allow this amalgamation to take place. Finally, let me say that money spent on good olive oil seems to me the most justifiable of all culinary expenses.

Orange flower water

You will find this fragrant liquid, distilled from orange blossoms, at Arab and Greek food shops. A bottle will last you a long time; the taste and scent add a special quality to various recipes in this book. See note on page 170.

Pomegranate juice

When this is mentioned I refer to the concentrated syrup made of sour pomegranate juice which you can buy from Middle Eastern shops. Although it contains sugar, the tartness of its flavour is fascinating. Lately, in our kitchen, we have rather fallen in love with it. A little goes a long way. We added a teaspoon to a salad dressing the other day; the result was thrilling.

Rose water

Don't think of 'Turkish delight'; the addition of a small quantity of this distillation from rose petals does not make a dish sickly but romantic. In Cyprus it is always added to Christmas cakes, but there are many other uses for it, as you will discover. See note on page 170.

Spices

Spices play an even more vital part than herbs in Middle Eastern cookery. I have to admit that unspiced food tends to seem insipid to me nowadays, and I would find cooking without spices a bore. We British, with our occasional pinches of nutmeg or cinnamon, have a lot to learn.

Different countries have different spice preferences; the Lebanese are very fond of allspice and also of a mixture of one third cayenne, one third paprika and one third cinnamon. The Greeks are fond of cinnamon as are the Cypriots who also have a great love of cumin. And so on. . . .

Allspice
Also known as pimento and Jamaica pepper, this is called 'allspice' because it unites the flavours of clove, cinnamon and nutmeg.

Cayenne or chilli pepper
You can grind your own from dried red chillis, but this is fiery stuff to handle. In cooking, too, treat it with caution, tasting after each small pinch.

Cinnamon
Probably the most popular of spices, it is used in both savoury and sweet dishes. Often a 'stick' or piece of bark is required for a recipe; at other times, ground (powdered) cinnamon is specified.

Clove
It will always have associations with bread sauce for me, which detracts a little from the romance of its powerful aroma. Be moderate with cloves. They are usually employed whole, but sometimes ground cloves are needed.

Coriander seeds
Whole, crushed or powdered, coriander seeds appear in quite a lot of recipes. They are the distinguishing feature of the Cyprus *Afelia* recipes (see pages 108 and 137).

Cumin (*artisia* in Cyprus)
This is my favourite spice. The smell is ravishing. The Cypriots claim that their *artisia* (so important in *Tavas*, see page 135) is different from cumin, but I can find no evidence for this. I buy the seeds and grind them in the food processor, but it is also available in powder form.

Cumin, black
These aromatic seeds (*Nigella sativa*) are actually nothing to do with cumin. They are used on sweet cakes and breads in Cyprus and Lebanon, and the Lebanese flavour Haloumi cheese with them.

Nutmeg
This is not very often required. When it is, grind it yourself. The powder loses its flavour very quickly.

Peppercorns, black
These are absolutely essential. In almost every recipe of the very many including pepper, freshly ground black pepper is what is required. Only when you do not want the pristine whiteness of a dish to look speckled should you resort to the white pepper which I have always stigmatized as 'sneezing powder'.

Saffron

This is the most expensive spice in the world because millions of crocus stamens are needed to produce quite a small quantity. There are fake saffrons about, so buy a reliable brand. The delicate threads should be pounded and soaked to bring out their scent and colour. Turmeric (see below) also gives colour, but is no substitute.

Sesame seeds

These delicious seeds are widely used in the Middle East: on breads and cakes, in *halva*, and, of course, for tahini (see below).

Sumac

This interesting spice is not widely known outside the Middle East. It has an attractive lemony taste, and is good sprinkled on meat for grilling, on chicken . . . and on fried eggs! It is sometimes used in *fattoush* (see page 110).

Turmeric

Often used for colouring foods (particularly rice) instead of saffron which is so expensive. However, it imparts a pungent aroma of its own as well as a bright yellow colour.

Tahini (in Arabic, Tahina)

This is an oily paste made from toasted sesame seeds. It should be thick, but over a period it tends to separate and requires blending before use. In Britain, you can now buy it from many large supermarkets as well as from health food stores and shops specializing in Middle Eastern provisions.

I have a vegetarian friend in Cyprus who buys tahini in half-gallon jars and uses it as a 'spread' (rather like peanut butter). However its most frequent use is in a sauce (see page 158) and in various dips for mezé.

Tomato

This seems a good place to describe a unique Cyprus contribution to cookery. When you require tomatoes to merge into a dish, cut off into a dish, cut off the stalk end, with any tough pith. Then grate on the large mesh of your cheese grater. (You will end up with a handful of tomato skin which you throw away.) This saves peeling the tomatoes and – more important – reduces them instantly to the texture you want.

Yogurt

This wonderful food recurs constantly in the course of this book, accompanied by my enthusiastic comments. Why don't you make your own, as suggested and described by Arto der Haroutunian? For the 'starter' he mentions, use ordinary commercial *plain* yogurt. I also give his instructions for stabilizing yogurt, for cooking.

'Although yogurt can be purchased commercially I strongly recommend that you make your own at home following the simple method below. There is no need to go to the expense of purchasing "yogurt makers" that manufacturers constantly tempt one with.

    1.2 litres/2 pints milk
    1 soupspoon yogurt – the
        starter (culture of the
        bacteria *Bulgaris*)

Bring the milk to the boil in a saucepan and when the froth rises turn off the heat.

Allow the milk to cool to the point where you can dip your finger in, and count up to 15 or, if you have a thermometer, where the temperature registers 45°C or 115°F.

Beat the spoon of yogurt in a cup, add a tablespoon of the warm milk, beat vigorously and pour into the milk. Empty the milk into an earthenware or glass bowl and stir for a minute. Cover the bowl with a large plate and wrap in a towel or tea towel. Place in a warm place, e.g. near a radiator or in an airing cupboard and do not disturb for about 10 hours. Remove the wraps and place the covered bowl in the refrigerator.

The yogurt is now ready to use. It can be kept for up to a week in the fridge. If using this yogurt as a 'starter' for a new batch then use it within three days (after this the balance of the bacteria in the culture alters and the quality of the new yogurt will be poorer).

To stabilize yogurt
If you are to use yogurt in hot dishes such as soups, sauces or stews, which require boiling it is necessary to stabilize it first otherwise it will curdle.
Either:
Stir a tablespoon of flour into a little water until you have a smooth paste and add to the yogurt before you heat it.
Or:
Beat an egg into the yogurt before cooking.

Note: Once the yogurt has been stabilized and boiled it cannot be used as a "starter" as the bacteria dies at a high temperature.'

BIBLIOGRAPHY

Soraya Antonius, *Simple Arab Cooking* (unpublished).
Arabella Boxer, *Mediterranean Cookbook*, Penguin, 1983.
Elizabeth David, *A Book of Mediterranean Food*, Penguin Books, 1955.
Alan Davidson, *A Kipper with My Tea*, Macmillan, 1988.
Gilli Davies, *The Taste of Cyprus*, Interworld Publications Ltd, 1990.
Arto der Haroutunian, *Middle Eastern Cookery*, Pan Books, 1983.
Ada Karaoglan, *A Gourmet's Delight*, Dar An-Nahar, Beirut, 1969.
Tess Mallos, *The Complete Middle East Cookbook*, Lansdowne Press, Sydney, 1983.
Theonie Mark, *Greek Islands Cooking*, Batsford, 1978.
George N. Rayess, *Rayess' Art of Lebanese Cooking*, Librairie du Liban, Beirut, 1966.
Claudia Roden, *A New Book of Middle Eastern Food*, Penguin, 1986.
Amaranth Sitas, *Kopiaste*, Cyprus, 1968.
Joyce M. Stubbs, *The Home Book of Greek Cookery*, Faber and Faber, 1963.

INDEX

Aboukht 27
The Adventurous Fish Cook [G Lassalle]
    129, 130
Afelia
  pork 137
  vegetable 108, 109
Africa, North 29
Aghia Varvara 84
allspice 184
amar ad-din 172
Amathus 84
anari 176, 180
Anginares 92–94, 109
Anginares ala polita 92
Anginares me Avgolemono 94
Anginares me Koukia 94
Antonius, Soraya 110, 153, 177
Apithia se Krassi 167
apricot cream 172
apricot with lamb chops 138
Archipelago Restaurant 84
Aristidou, John 51
Armenia 118
Armenian recipes 27, 39, 118, 138
Arnaki me Filo 128
Arni Fricasse 136
Arni Kleftiko 127, 136
Arni Palikari 127
Arni psito 126

artichoke (globe)
  afelia 109
  braised 92
  with broad bean 94
  with egg/lemon 94
  with lamb 117
artichoke (Jerusalem) 92
artisia 136, 185
Assyria 112
aubergine
  cooked in oven 96
  Imam fainted 95
  moussaka, meat 140
  moussaka, meatless 97
  Sultan's delight 98
  to stuff 86
Avga me Horta 44
avgolemono
  sauce 158 *and* 33, 91, 94, 136, 151
  soup 32, 34
avgotarakho 23
avocado with tahini 21
Ayva kompostu 166

Baba Ghannouj 20, 98
Ba'dounis bi-tahina 117
Baghdad 154
baharat 160
baklava 164

ba'leh 116
Balik kebabi 49
Bamies Yahni 102
Barbunya kağitta 50
basil 116
Basturma 27
Batata bil-Toum 104
Batata mahshi 103
Batata mutabbaleh 121
bay leaf 181
Bayd Hamine 41, 42
Bayd ma' akbad al dajaj 45
Bayd Mahshi 42
Bazergan 112
beans
   black eyed in tomato sauce 77
   black eyed bean stew 77
   broad bean 78, 99, 100, 137
   broad bean dip 22
   broad beans fried 99
   broad bean with artichoke 94
   fava bean 75, 76
   green (french) bean with meat 134
   haricot beans boiled 74
   haricot beans soup 36
   haricot beans stewed 75
   kidney beans casserole 78
   kidney beans salad 114
   white bean salad 113
beef 124, 133
   dried, with fenugreek/garlic 27
   in pancakes 144
   rissoles 145
   with cherries 139
beetroot 121, 122
blette 69, 77
brains
   fried 147
   with lemon 148
bread 177-179
   Arab 110, 177, 178
   Arab, recipe 178
   Cypriot 177
   pitta 177, 178
   with salad 110
brigands 127
Britain 30, 55, 61, 67, 111, 121, 129,

   131, 145, 163, 164
broad beans 22, 78, 99, 100, 137
Budugov miss 138
bulgur 67
burghul
   and parsley salad 111, 112
   and yogurt soup 33
   in tomato 88
   kibbeh 71-74
   pilaf 68, 70
   Prue's steamed 69
   salad 112
   with lentils 80
butter 179
butter, to clarify 179

Cayenne 184
Çerkes Tavuğu 152
chard 69, 77
cheese 179-181
   Anari 176, 180
   Cheddar 106, 108
   Feta 26, 52, 97, 106, 117, 128, 180
   Haloumi 27, 34, 108, 180
   Kasseri 180
   Kafalotiri 101, 106, 128, 144, 180
   Labneh 180, 181, 122, 176
   Mizithra 176, 181
   Parmesan 101, 106, 144
Chelau 64, 140
Chelau ta Dig 65
cherries, stewed with meat 139
cherry water-ice 168
chick pea 79
   balls 24, 25
   hummus 19
chicken 129, 134, 149-156
   Circassian 152
   in envelopes 155
   kebab 131
   liver, with egg 45
   mouloukhia 150
   paprika 154
   pilaf 154
   Soraya 153
   with egg/lemon sauce 157
chicory 137

chilli 24, 25, 184
chips (potato) 103
Çilbir 43
Çilekli dondurma 168
cinnamon 185
'Clean Monday' 83, 84
clove 185
compôtes 165–168
coriander, fresh 115
coriander seeds 108, 109, 115, 185
Costi, Androula 34, 106, 145
courgette
    baked in tahini 100
    rissoles 101
    to stuff 86
    with eggs 46
    with lamb 137
crock pot 134
cucumber with yogurt 120
cumin 135, 136, 185
cuttlefish stew 57
Cypriot recipes 20, 26–38, 30–33,
        35–37, 44, 50, 58, 70, 74, 75, 77,
        91, 94, 96, 102, 106, 117, 120,
        126, 127, 130, 131, 134, 135,
        144, 145, 147, 148, 162, 173
Cyprus, food and cookery 18, 19, 23,
        29, 50, 51, 52, 62, 71, 73, 82–85,
        92, 102, 103, 106–108, 120,
        123–125, 127, 131, 132, 136,
        140, 144, 158, 159, 172, 176

Dajaj bil-bahar al-helou 154
Davidson, Alan 124, 125
dhaniya 115
dill 182
Dobson, Meric 150, 154
dolma 85
dolmades 85
Domata Salsa 159
Domates Salatasi 119
Domato Soupa 38
dried fruit 170–172
Dukkous al-tamata 160

Easter 29, 30, 85
Easter soup 30

Efkolo Kalamari 55
egg
    hard-boiled 41
    stuffed 42
    with chicken livers 45
    with fresh greens 44
    with marrow/courgette 46
    with vegetables 44
    with yogurt 43
eggah, 41, 46, 47
Egyptian recipes 19–22, 28, 41, 42, 62,
        75, 88, 114, 150
Elies Marinates 26
elioti 177

Falafel 24, 25, 79
Fassolada 74
Fassolada Yahni 75
Fassolakia me Kreas 134
Fassolia Soupa 36
Fattoush 110
Fava 22
fava bean 75, 76
fennel 182
Feta
    dressed 27
    in salad 117
    in spinach pie 106
    with aubergine 96
    with lamb 128
    with prawn 52
filo pastry 106, 107, 128
fish
    anchovies with rice 53
    cuttlefish stew 57
    'Fisherman's' 54
    fish-roe dip 23
    fish-roe rissoles 59
    Greek 51
    kebab 49
    Kyria Eftychia's Octopus Stew 56
    marinated 58
    prawns with Feta 52
    red mullet in foil 50
    simple squid 55
    soup 35
    squid salad 58

squid stew 57
trout Maryland 50
with tahini 48
flaounes 177
fruit 165–172
Ful Medammes 75, 76
Ful Nabed 22

Garithes me Feta 52
garlic 181
  sauces 161, 162
  with potatoes 104
Georgia, USSR 152
glysterida 116
grapes, frosted 169
Greece, food and cookery 29, 105, 118, 124, 144
Greek recipes 21, 23, 30, 32, 33, 35, 36, 38, 51, 52, 55, 56, 58, 59, 74, 75, 92, 94, 97, 99, 101, 104–106, 117, 120, 126–128, 130, 133, 134, 136, 138, 140, 141, 151, 158, 159, 161, 162, 166, 167, 169, 172, 173
Grigson, Jane 132
Gulf States recipe 160

Haloumi 27, 34, 108, 180, 185
Haloumi grilled and fried 27
Haloumi psito i tiganito 27
Hamsi tavasi 53
hare *stifado* 133
haricot beans
  boiled 74
  salad 74
  soup 36
  stewed 75
Haroutunian, Arto der 178, 187, 188
Hirino me Kithonia 138
Hiromeri 28
Horiatiki salata 117
Hosaf 170
Hrisomila Peltes 172
Hummus bi-tahina 19, 20
hummus soup 35
hummus with tahini 19, 20
Hunkar Beyendi 98

Imam Bayildi 95
Iranian recipes 64, 65, 139
Iraqi recipe 154
Italy 123
Izmir Koftesi 143
Izmir Kompostu 171

Jerusalem artichoke 92
Jordan 111

Kabis Flayfileh Helweh 123
Kafta bil-saniya 141
Kakavia 35
Kalamari Salata 58
Kalamari Yahni 57
Kanellonia 144
kasseri 180
katayfi 164
kebab
  chicken 131
  fish 49
  lamb 129
  pork 129
  sausage 131
  veal 129
kefalotiri 101, 106, 128, 144, 180
Keftedes 145
Khoresht e-albaloo 139
Khoshaf 170
Kibbeh Nayeh 71–74
Kibbeh bil-saniyeh 72–74
kid 124
Kidneys in lemon sauce 147
Kidneys with pomegranate juice 146
kidney bean
  casserole 78
  salad 114
Kilawi bi-asir al-rumman 146
Kilawi ma' al-hamud 147
A Kipper with My Tea [A Davidson] 124, 125
Kirazli dondurma 168
Kirkuk 154
kleftiko 127, 136
Kolokythia Keftedes 101
Komposto 165
Konya 125

Korumb Mahshi 88
Kotopoulo me Avgolemono 151
Koukia Tiganita 99
koulouri 177
Koupé 71
Koupepia 86, 91
Kousa bi-tahina 100
Kousa ma' bayd bil-furn 46
Kyria Eftychia's Octopus Stew 56

Laban bil-bayd, 43
labneh 43, 122, 176, recipe 180, 181
ladies' fingers 102
lahana 69, 77
lamb
  'bandit style' 127
  braised 135
  casserole with cumin 135
  chops with apricot 138
  fricassée 136
  in filo pastry 128
  kebab 129
  moussaka 141
  meat loaf 141, 142
  roast 126
  roast whole 124, 125
  soup 30, 31
  with cherries 139
  with green beans 134
  with pork sausage 131, 132
  with potato, stuffed 103
lamb's brain 147, 148
lamb's head soup 31
lamb's kidney 146, 147
lamb's liver 148
Latholemono 162 *and* 50, 52, 115, 118, 120
Lebanese recipes 24, 38, 39, 43, 45, 48, 54, 66, 71-74, 80, 89, 100, 103, 104, 110, 111, 114, 117, 121, 123, 130, 141, 142, 146, 148, 153, 155, 170, 173, 174, 175
Lebanon, food and cookery 62, 111, 112, 161, 163
leek 101
  pie 107
  salad 120

with rice 105
lemon
  and egg sauce 33, 91, 94, 136, 151
  and egg soup 32, 34
  and oil sauce 50, 52, 115, 118, 120, 162
  to pickle 153
  sorbet 169
lemon sorbet 169
Lent 83
lentil
  balls 25
  dip 22
  Lassalle 79, 80
  salad 114
  soup 39
  with rice or burghul 80
lettuce, cooked 136
Lévi-Strauss, Claude 124
Limassol 26, 29, 52, 83, 101, 124, 126
limoni serbeti 169
liver, chicken with egg 45
liver with vinegar 148
London 18, 133, 149, 158, 164
Lounza 28
Louvana 37
Louvia mavromatica me domates 77
Louvia mavromatica me lahana 77

Madzounabour 39
mahallepi 173
Mahshi malfouf bil-zayt 89
mallow 150
Mamouniyeh 175
Manitaria 109
marinades for kebab 128–131
marrow with eggs 46
Maryland Restaurant 51
mastic 173
Mayeritsa 29, 30
meat-ball soup 32
meat-eating in the Middle-East 27, 28, 124–145
meat loaf 141, 142
meat preserved 27, 28
meat rissoles 145
meat with pancakes 144

Melitzanes sto Fourno 96
Menemen 44
Merjimek koftesi 26
mezé 18-28
  avocado with tahini 20
  beef, dried 27
  broad bean dip 22
  carrot dip 21
  falafel 24, 25
  hummus 19, 20
  lentil balls 25
  lentil dip 21
  marinated olives 26
  pork fillet, smoked 28
  pork leg, smoked 28
  red lentil dip 23
  taramosalata 23
Miala me Limoni 148
Miala Tiganita 147
Middle-East, food and cookery 18, 19,
  53, 61, 62, 82-85, 103, 106, 110,
  115, 119, 120, 123-125, 129,
  133, 140, 146, 148, 158, 164,
  165, 170, 172
Middle-Eastern Cookery [A der
  Haroutunian] 178, 187, 188
mint 182
mizithra 176, 181
Moghli 174
Mouloukhia ala dajaj 150
Mousakhan 155
moussaka
  meat 140, 141
  meatless 97, 100
Moussaka horis Kreas 97
Muhallabiyeh 173
Mujaddarah 80, 110
mushroom 88, 109

Nicosia 24, 84, 150, 153
nutmeg 185
nuts 183
nuts in meat loaf 142

octopus stew 56
offal 145-149

oil and lemon sauce 50, 52, 115, 118,
  120, 162
oil, olive 183
okra 102
okra stew 102
Oktopodi Yahni tis Kyrias Eftychias 56
Old Mill Restaurant 51
olives marinated 26
olive oil 183
'onion juice' 129, 130
onions, to stuff 86
oranges in syrup 167
orange flower water 174, 183
oregano 182

Palikari 127
Panaghia tou Asinou 85
pancakes with meat 144
panna 132
parsley 116, 182
  and burghul salad 111, 112
  and tahini salad 117
pasta 39
pasticcio 144
pastry 106-108
Patsia 31
Patata keftedes 104
peach compôte 166
pears i wine 167
peppercorns 185
pepper, white 99
peppers, green 135, 143
peppers, sweet 122
  pickled 123
  to stuff 87
pie
  leek 107
  spinach 106, 107
pilaf
  chicken 154
  burghul 68, 70
pine nuts 183
Piyaz 113
pligouri 67
pomegranate juice 146, 184
pork 124, 125, 129, 134
  Afelia 137

rissoles 145
smoked fillet 28
smoked leg 28
with quince 138
Portokalia Syropata 167
potatoes 103–105, 109
   Afelia 109
   rissoles 104
   spiced 121
   stuffed 103
   with garlic 104
pourgouri 67
Pourgouri Pilafi 70, 136, 137
Prassopitta 107
Prassorizo 105
prawns with Feta 52
Provence 123
Psara, Mr 83
Psari Marinato 58
Psari Plaki 51
Psomi 177
puff pastry 106, 108
pulses 74–81 *see also* beans, lentils,
   chick peas
Purdah Pilau 154
purslane 44, 45, 110, 116

quince compôte 166
quince with pork 138

rabbit 133
red mullet in foil 50
Revythia me Tahini 35
rice
   cream 173
   for fish 66
   steamed 64, 65
   to cook (3 ways) 62–64
   with almonds/dates 67
   with aniseed 174
   with leeks 105
   with lentils 80
   with milk 173
   with spinach 105
rigani 51, 119, 182
rissoles 59, 101, 145
Rizogalo 173

Roc bi-halib 173
rocket 116, 119
rokka 116
rose water 184
rosemary 126, 182
Rothakina Komposta 166
Ruz bil-loz wa bil-tammar 67
Ruz lil-asmak 66

saffron 186
salad
   burghul 112
   burghul and parsley 111
   cucumber with yogurt 120
   kidney bean 114
   leek 120
   lentil 114
   mixed 122
   parsley and tahini 117
   pickled pepper 123
   pink 121
   rice 115
   spiced potato 121
   spinach and yogurt 118
   tomato 119
   village 117
   white bean 113
salad dressing 163
salad herbs 115, 116
Salata Jazar 21
Salata Turlu-Turlu 122
Salata wardiyeh 121, 122
Salatit Ades 114
Salatit Loubia Hmra 114
Salsa Avgolemono 33, 91, 94, 136, 151,
   158
Samak bi-tahina 48
sauces 157–163
   béchamel 106, 107
   egg and lemon 33, 91, 94, 136, 151,
      158
   garlic 161, 162
   oil and lemon 50, 52, 115, 118, 120,
      162
   tahini 158
   tomato 159, 160
   yogurt 162

sausage 131, 132, 143
sausage skins 132
Savvides, Rebecca 75, 96
Sayyadieh 54
sesame seeds 186
Seymour, Ian 85
Seymour, Prue 69, 112
Sheftalia 131
Shish Kebabi 129
Shomin 118
Shurbat ades ma sha'riya 39
Shurbat banadoura ma' shabitt 38
Skordalia 161
Smyrna 40, 171
Smyrna sausage 143
Snow, Charles 24, 25
Soda bil-khall 148
sorbets 168, 169
Soudzoukakia 143
soup 29–40
    burghul and yogurt 33
    cucumber and yogurt 40
    Easter 30
    egg and lemon 32
    fish 35
    Granny Williamson's 40
    haricot bean 36
    hummus 35
    lamb's head 31
    lentil and vermicelli 39
    meatball 32
    split pea 37
    tomato 38
    yogurt 39
Soupies Yahni 57
Souvlakia 131
Spain 123
Spanakopitta 106
Spanakorizo 105
spices 184–186
spinach 105–108
spinach pie 106, 107
spinach with rice 105
squid 55, 57, 58
Stafylia zaharomena 169
stew, meat 133–140
stew with onions 133

Stifado 133
stock cubes 102
strawberry water-ice 168
Sultan's Delight 98
Sultan Ibrahim 50
sumac 45, 110, 186
sweet course 164–176
    cherry water-ice 168
    dried fruit salad 170
    frosted grapes 169
    honey and cheese 176
    honey and yogurt 176
    lemon sorbet 169
    orange water-ice 169
    oranges in syrup 167
    peach compôte 166
    pears in wine 167, 168
    quince compôte 166
    rice cream 173
    rice milk 173
    rice with aniseed 174
    semolina 175
    Smyrna fig compôte 171
    strawberry water-ice 168
Syria 111, 112
Syrian recipes 112

Tabbouleh 111, 112
tahini 186
    and parsley salad 117
    in meatloaf 142
    sauce 158
    with avocado 21
    with courgette 100
    with fish 48
    with hummus
tahiniyeh 19, 20, 158
tahinosalata 20, 159
Talatouri 120, 155
Tarama Keftedes 59
Taramosalata 23
Tarator 161
Tas Kebabi 135
Tavas 135
tomato
    salad 119
    sauce 159, 160

soup 38
to grate 186
to stuff 87, 88
Trahanas 33, 34
Triandafillides, Mr and Mrs 29
Troodos Mountains 50, 85
trout Maryland 50, 51
Tsatsiki 120
Turkey, food and cookery 62, 65, 111,
    123, 165
Turkish recipes 25, 40, 43, 44, 49, 50,
    52, 53, 95, 98, 113, 119, 120,
    122, 129, 130, 135, 143, 152,
    161, 162, 166, 168, 170, 171
turmeric 186
tzavar 67

veal 129
vegetables, stuffed 85–92

vegetarians 25, 82, 124
vine leaves, stuffed 90, 91
Vizakia 85

Williamson, Mrs 40

yellow split pea 37, 79
yemista 85, 86
yogurt
    and burghul soup 33
    marinade for kebab 130, 131
    sauce 162
    soup 39, 40
    to make 187, 188
    with cucumber 120
    with eggs 43
    with honey 176
Youvarlakia 32
yufka 106